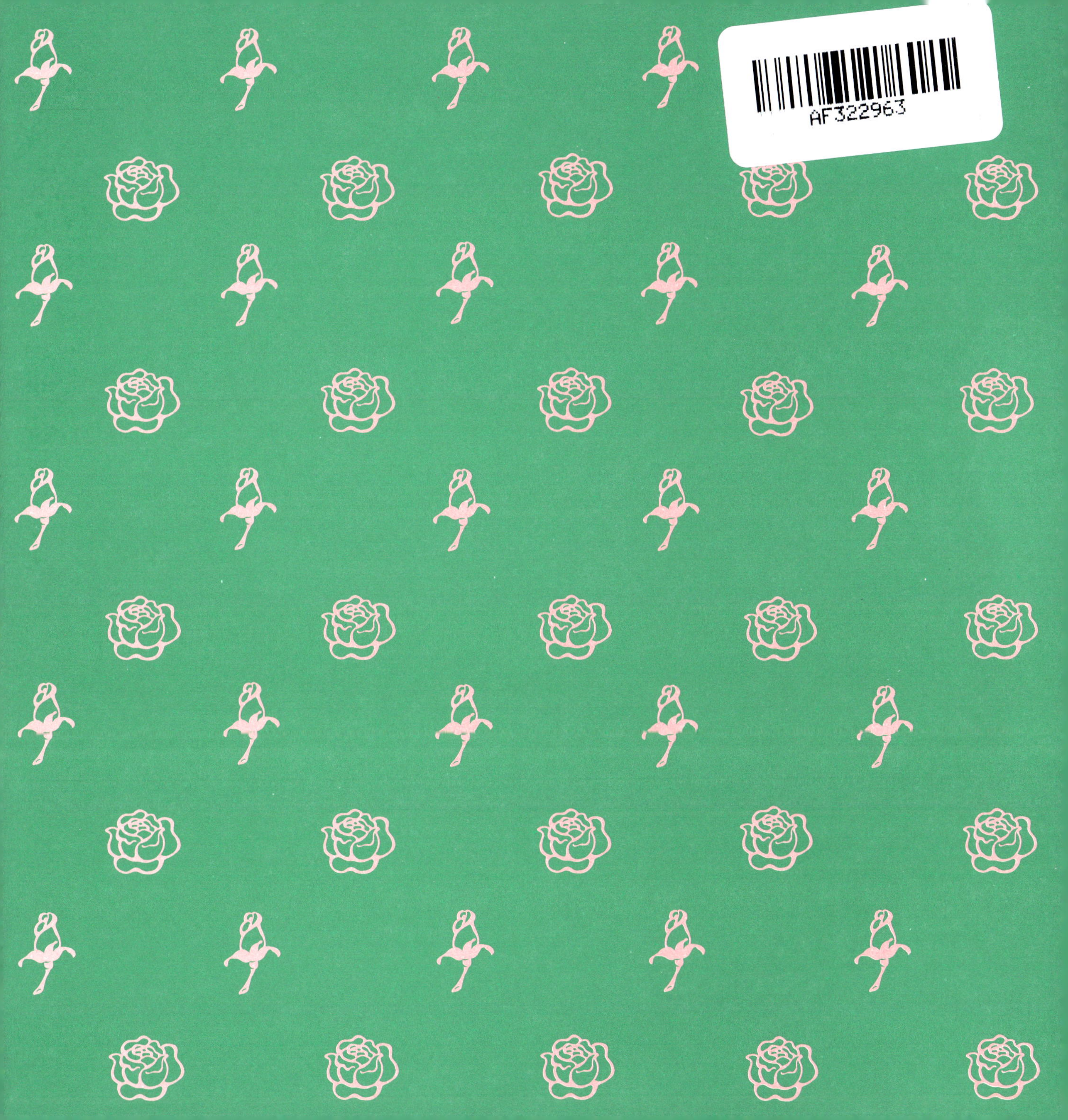

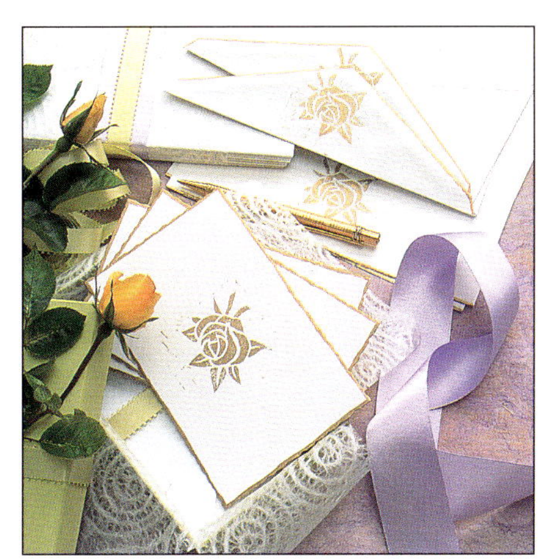

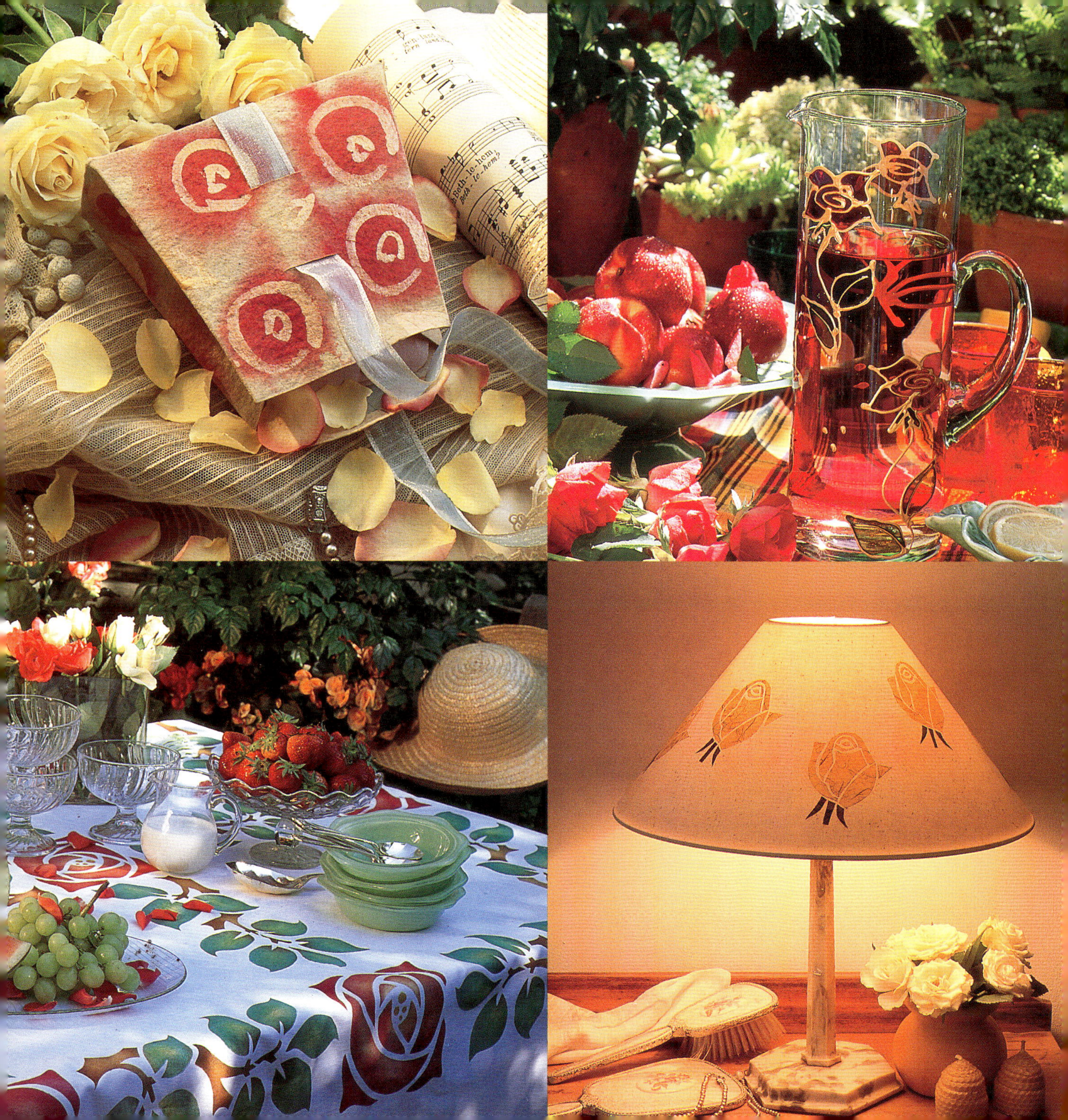

ROSES

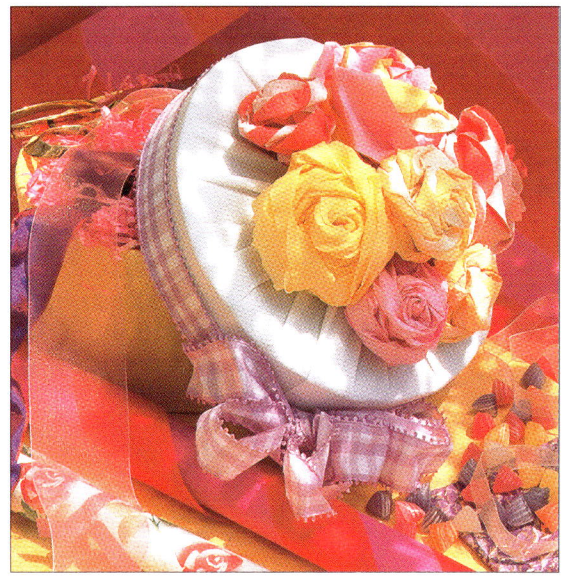

JOANNE RIPPIN

PHOTOGRAPHS BY MICHELLE GARRETT

LORENZ BOOKS
NEW YORK · LONDON · SYDNEY · BATH

This edition published in the UK in 1997 by Lorenz Books

This edition published in the USA in 1997 by Lorenz Books
27 West 20th Street
New York, NY 10011

LORENZ BOOKS are available for bulk purchase for
sales promotion and for premium use.
For details write or call the manager of special sales:
Lorenz Books, 27 West 20th Street,
New York, NY 10011. (212) 807-6739.

©1997 Anness Publishing Limited

Lorenz Books is an imprint of Anness Publishing Limited

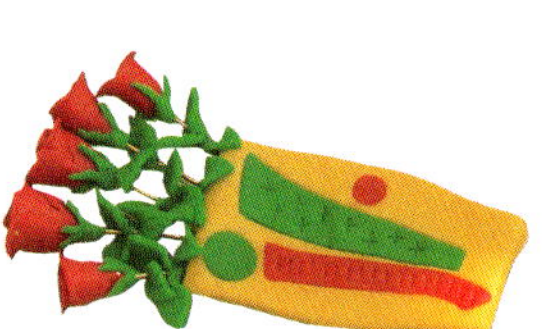

ISBN 1 85967 345 7

Publisher: Joanna Lorenz
Introduction by: Beverley Jollands
Designer: Lilian Lindblom
Photographer: Michelle Garrett
Step photography: Janine Hosegood
Illustrations: Lucinda Ganderton

Printed in China

1 3 5 7 9 10 8 6 4 2

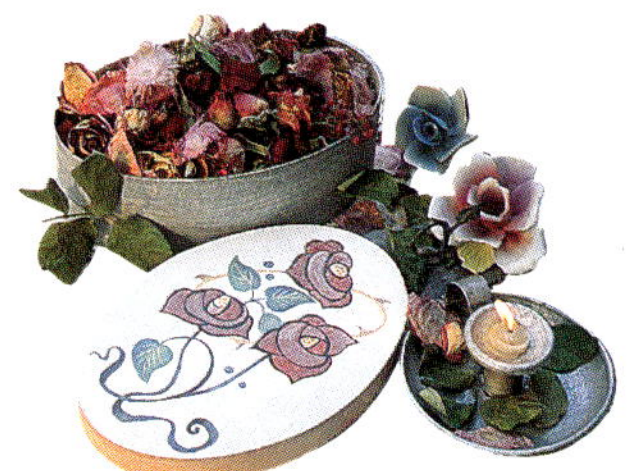

Contents

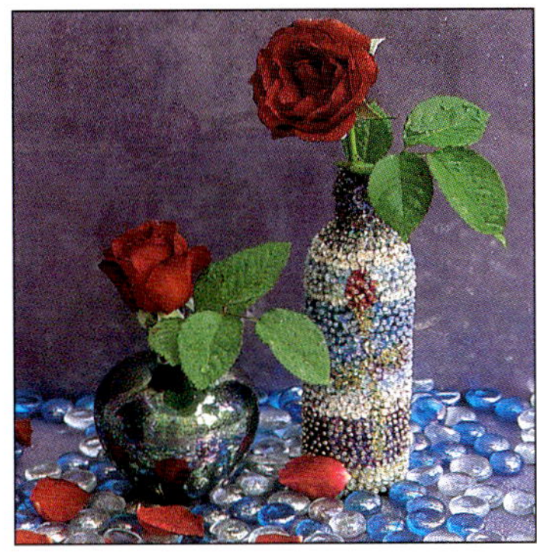

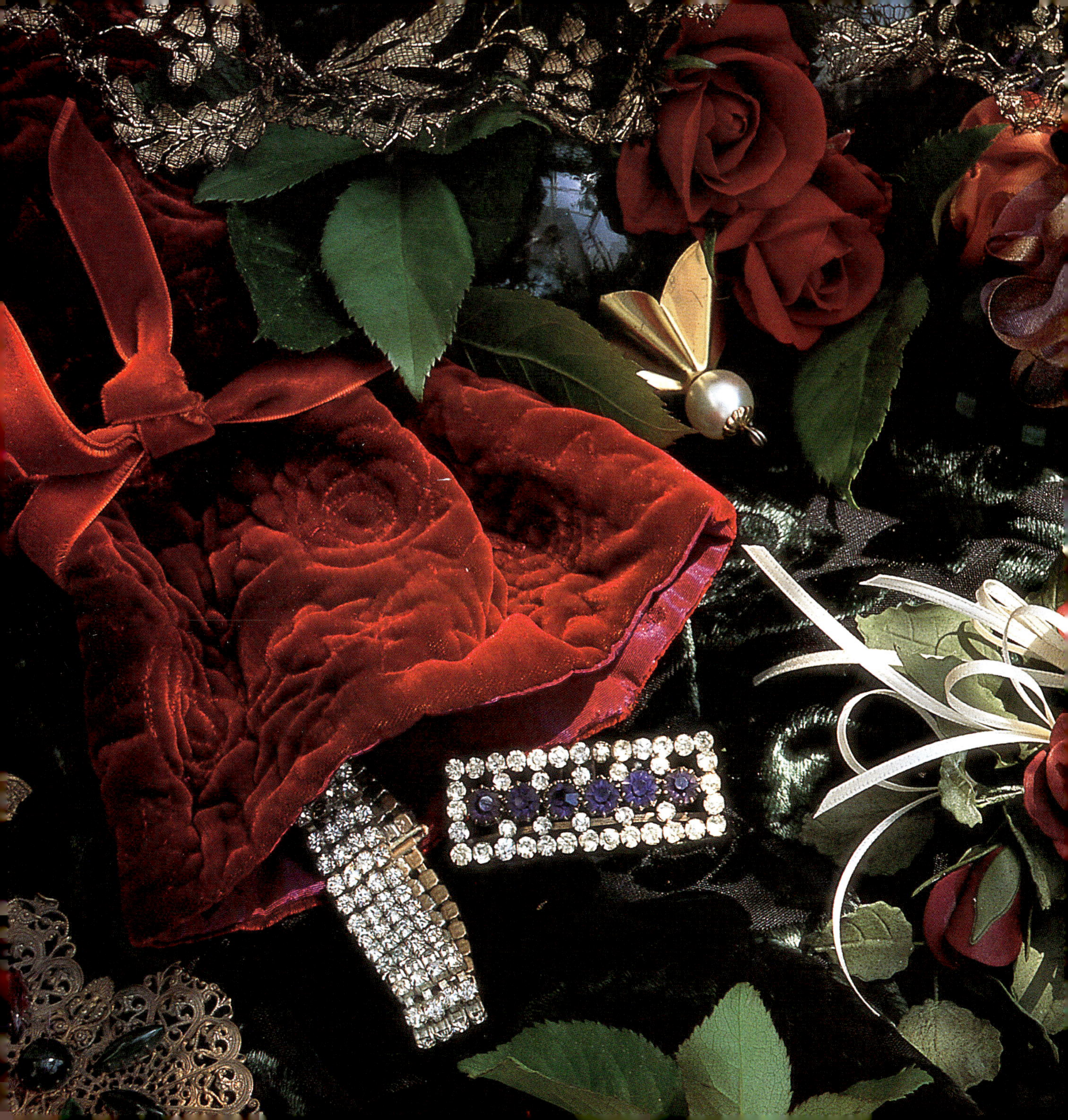

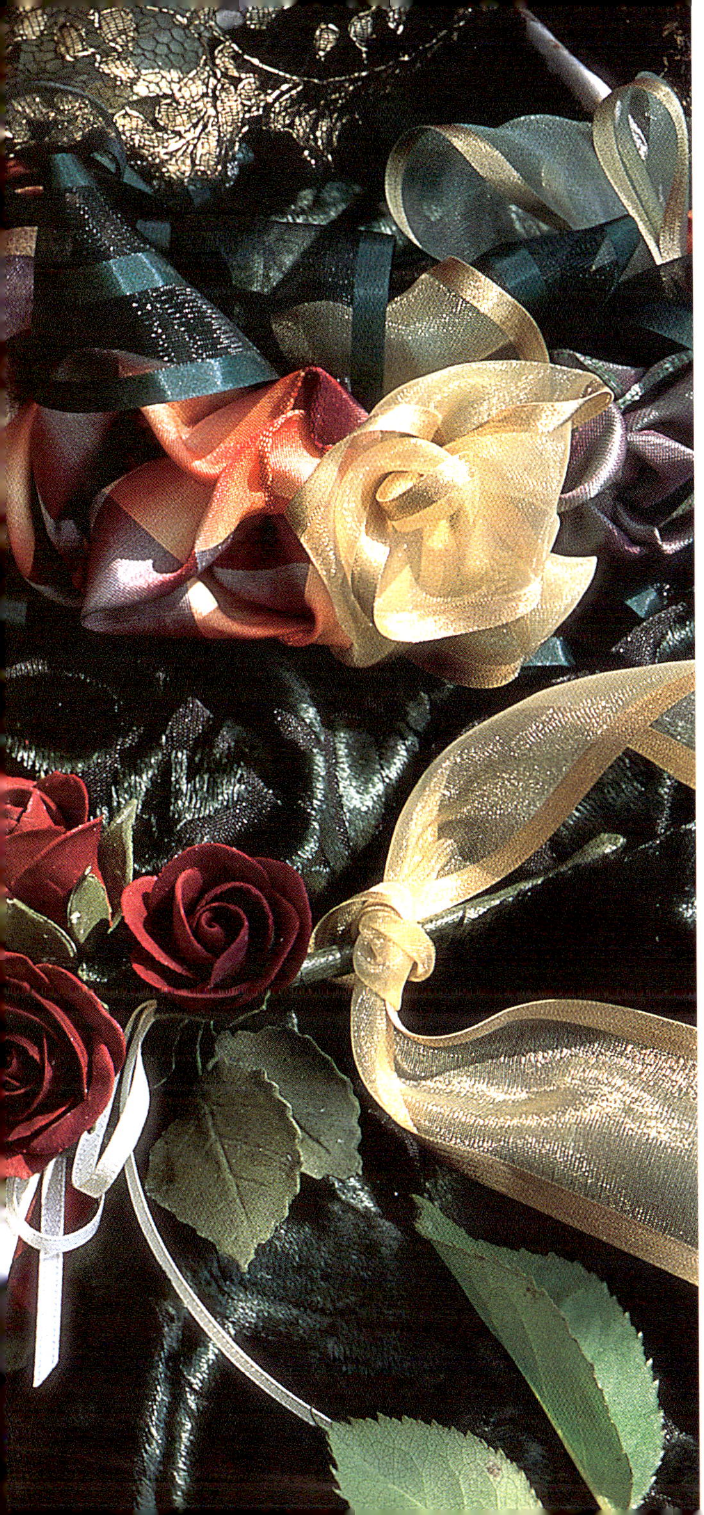

INTRODUCTION

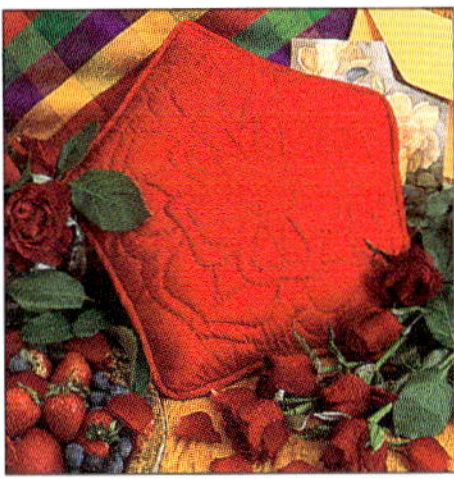

Of all decorative motifs, flowers are the first that spring to mind, and of all flowers the rose is paramount. Sappho eulogized it as the queen of flowers in the 6th century BC, and it has rarely lost its foremost place in the affections of gardeners, designers, painters, embroiderers, and everyone else who uses and appreciates flowers.

The cultivation of roses is very ancient. Minoan frescoes and gold jewelry of the 16th century BC are decorated with them. Both the Greeks and Romans loved them, and the coinage of ancient Rhodes was stamped with a rose. Partying Romans wore crowns of roses, and thousands of the flowers were strewn over tables, floors and streets. Decadent emperors arranged for them to drop from the ceiling over their guests in such quantities that at one banquet several diners are supposed to have suffocated in them. (The Victorian painter Alma-Tadema conjured up this voluptuous orgy in *The Roses of Heliogabalus* in 1888.)

For Christians, the white rose was an emblem of the Virgin Mary and thus of perfection. It appears in Gothic cathedrals in great rose windows such as those of York, Lincoln and Chartres. Devotional books were known

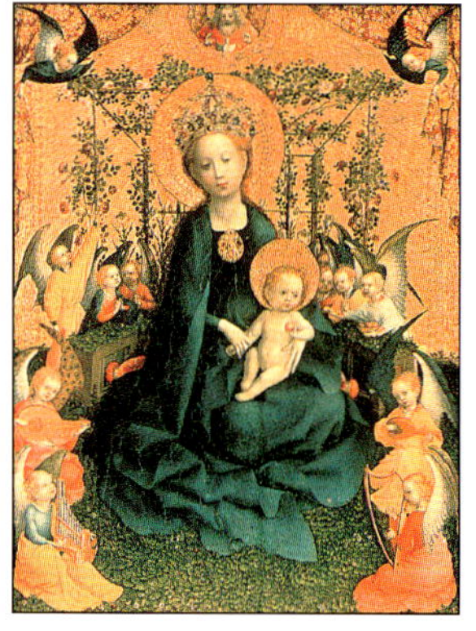

as *rosaria:* this extended first to the devotions themselves, and finally to the prayer beads that accompanied them. At the convent of St Theresa of Avila in Spain, rosary beads used by the faithful are still made from rose petals.

The rose stood for secrecy in the medieval world. Cupid, the legend went, had bribed the god of silence with a rose to keep quiet about the indiscretions of Venus. So roses were hung from the ceiling during secret talks, and the practice grew of carving roses over council tables and in confessionals. "*Sub rosa*" – or "under the rose" – meant something like "between you and me." This is possibly the origin of the Victorian ceiling rose.

The familiar Tudor rose, combining the red rose of Lancaster and the white rose of York, was a potent symbol of the peaceful union between these two warring factions. But when Elizabeth I came to the throne rose imagery

ran riot. She was flatteringly known as "the rose without a thorn" and her portraits are full of roses; apart from the real ones in her hand, they are embroidered all over her clothes and set in jewels around her neck. Contemporary domestic plasterwork and needlework across the country bloomed with roses in all their glory as a compliment to her.

Queen Elizabeth's era was a time of

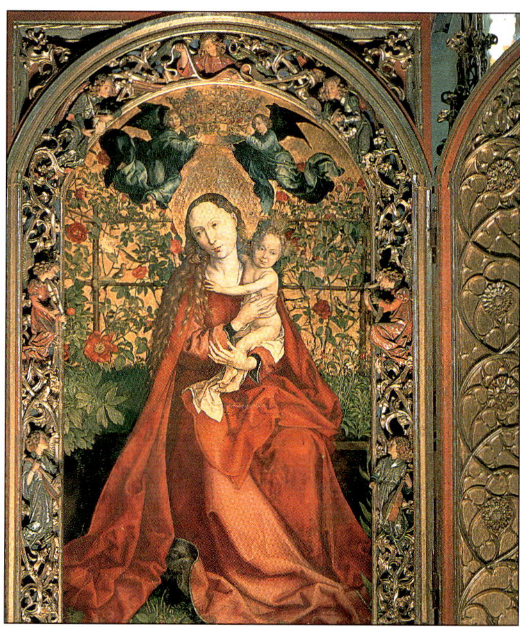

Top: One of the many works of art which show the Virgin Mary with her emblem – the rose.

Above: A painting on wood of the Virgin Mary in a rose arbor, by Martin Schongauer.

passionate gardening and plant discoveries, and flower paintings were fashionable. Decorators of houses and palaces commissioned flower pieces to fit over doors and mantels, while furniture was covered in floral marquetry copied from the detailed botanical paintings of the Dutch school – glorious mixed arrangements

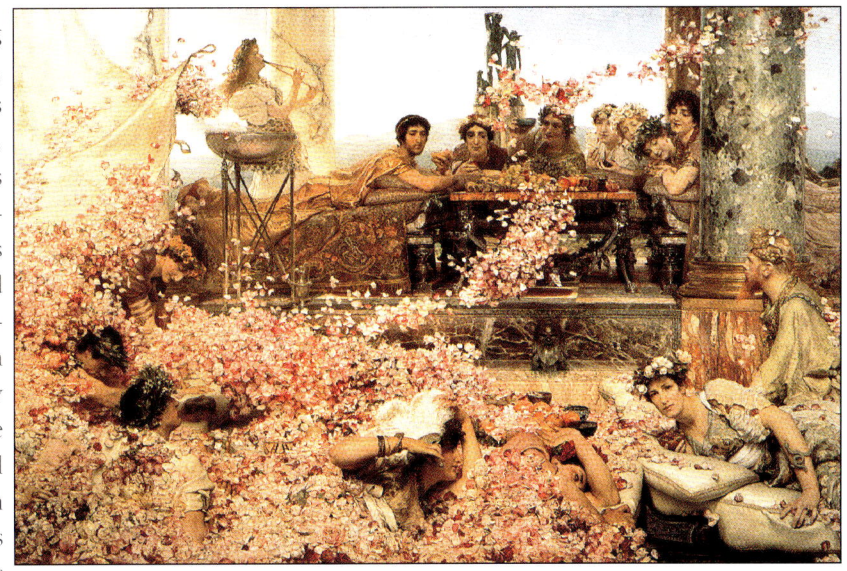

Above: Rose petals cascade from the ceiling in the famous painting by Sir Lawrence Alma-Tadema.

in which roses played a central role. Tapestries, damasks, Turkish carpets and upholstery were all covered in a profusion of flowers. For the next two hundred years flowers would continue to dominate interior design, from the delicate naturalism of Spitalfields silks and painted porcelain from factories like Bow, Chelsea and Derby, to wax flower arrangements under glass domes and the flamboyant cabbage roses on the carpet of a Victorian parlor. As a reaction against the floral decoration of the Victorians, designers like William Morris concentrated on simpler flowers such as daisies and larkspur. Morris cautioned fellow designers "to be shy of double flowers." He used single roses.

Roses lost out to more sinuous flower forms such as irises and tulips in the curving designs of Art Nouveau. However, Charles Rennie Mackintosh used a flat cut-out rose motif, derived from the work of Glasgow embroiderers, on chairs, doors, leaded glass and textiles. The same design can be found in the work of Beardsley and Voysey. It was so popular in France that it was named after the French designer, Paul Iribe. From 1918 until the end of the

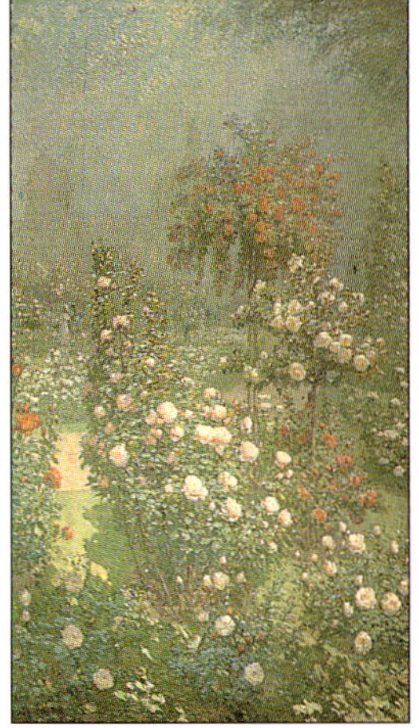

twenties, "la Rose Iribe" appeared everywhere on mass-produced fabrics and wallpapers. It is an ideal pattern for you to adapt in one of your own stenciled or embroidered designs.

Cottage gardeners have grown and loved roses for centuries, and they are an enduring theme in folk art. Stylized roses – together with castles – are the traditional decoration of British canal boats. In 19th-century America they were popular quilting motifs. A large central rose surrounded by branches of smaller flowers and buds was called "Whig Rose" or "Democrat Rose," depending on the political allegiance of the quilter.

Numerous artists have exploited the relationship between roses and romantic love. The Rococo decorations of Boucher and Fragonard spill over with roses, and the tangled roses in Burne-Jones' *Love Among the Ruins* recall the fable of the Sleeping Beauty surrounded by impenetrable briars. Victorian lovers sent elaborate Valentine cards garlanded with roses, and the romantic message is just as clear today. It is the perfect flower for a wedding, from little pink rosebuds in the bridesmaids' hair to a shower of rose petals in place of confetti. Make the most of its romantic associations before the big day too; decorate your own rose-stamped wedding stationery, or dress up a wedding gift with exuberant paper flowers.

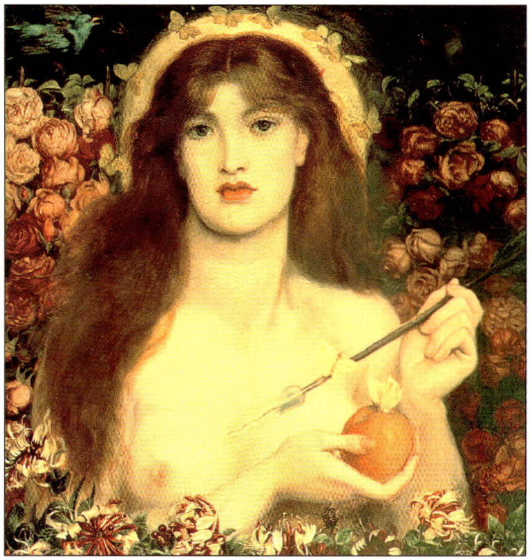

Top: A decorative panel depicting a traditional rose garden, by Ernest Quost.

Above: Rossetti's depiction of Venus, with roses – the flowers of love – in the background.

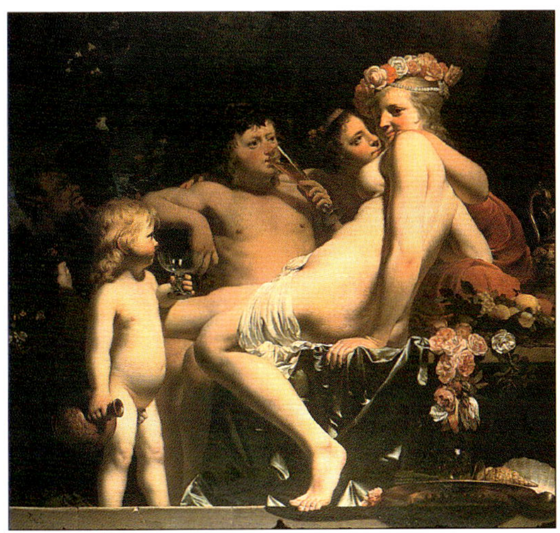

*Above: Bacchus and Love, surrounded by roses,
in a painting by Caesar Boetius van Everdingen.*

In recent decades, our renewed love affair with old roses, with their arching stems, rich pinks and mauves and intoxicating scents, has extended to a romantic, naturalistic use of roses as decoration. A jug of garden roses, or an informal hand-tied bouquet, has a fresher appeal than a formal arrangement of florists' blooms. Dried roses, bowls of potpourri and rose oil scent homes decorated with billowing nostalgic rose-printed fabrics and sponged tableware inspired by traditional chintz in old-fashioned colors. Soft, natural textures and combinations of delicate prints in patchwork or decoupage enhance this look.

The projects that follow have been influenced not just by the visual beauty of the rose, but by its delicacy and romance, the velvet texture of its petals and its rich and timeless symbolism. Make them for yourself, your home, or as gifts, or adapt them to suit your own ideas. If you have roses in your garden, they will be an inspiration.

Above: A rose wallpaper design by William Morris.

P A P E R   R O S E S   G I F T   B O X

To make a gift seem even more special, present it in this decorated box. The romantic roses make this perfect for a wedding present.

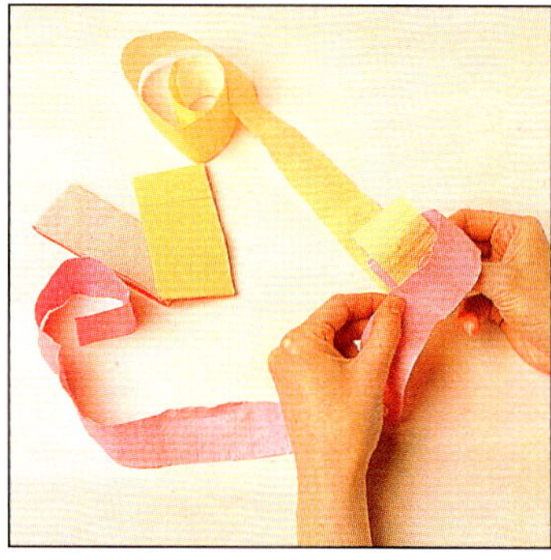

1 To make the roses, cut through the folded crêpe paper to make strips about 2 inches wide. Tape two strips at right angles to each other. Fold one over the other, to make an accordion.

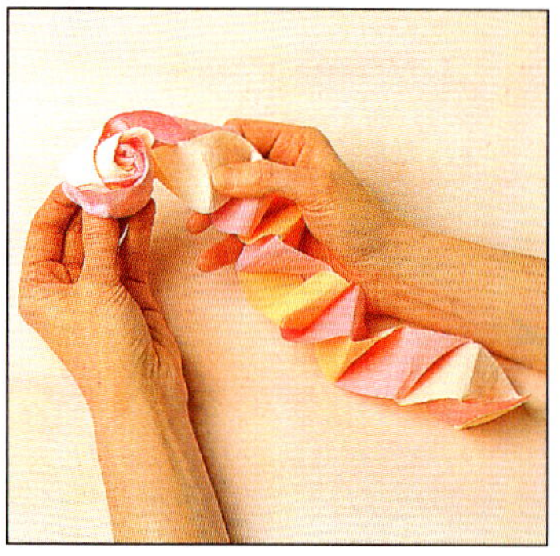

2 Holding the ends, stretch the accordion to its fullest extent and wind it up, twisting to get a rose shape. Tape the ends of the strips into a "stalk." Make several roses of different colors and sizes.

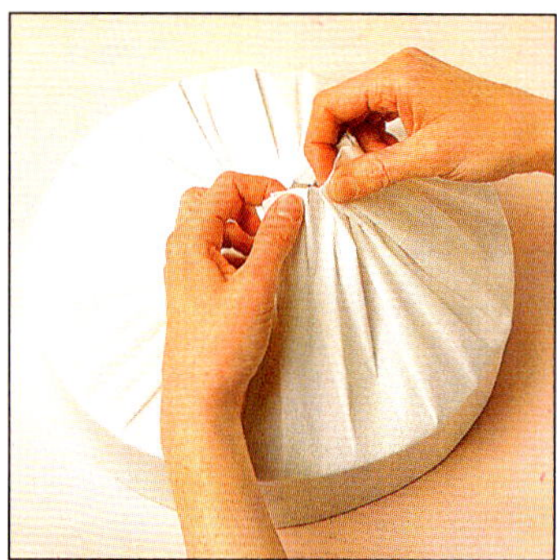

3 Cover the box and lid with crêpe paper, neatly pleating the fullness and sticking it down so it is as flat as possible in the center of the lid.

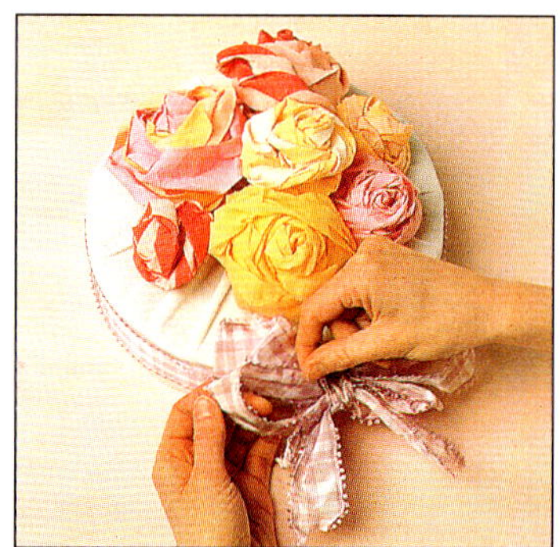

4 Glue the roses on top. Finish with a ribbon.

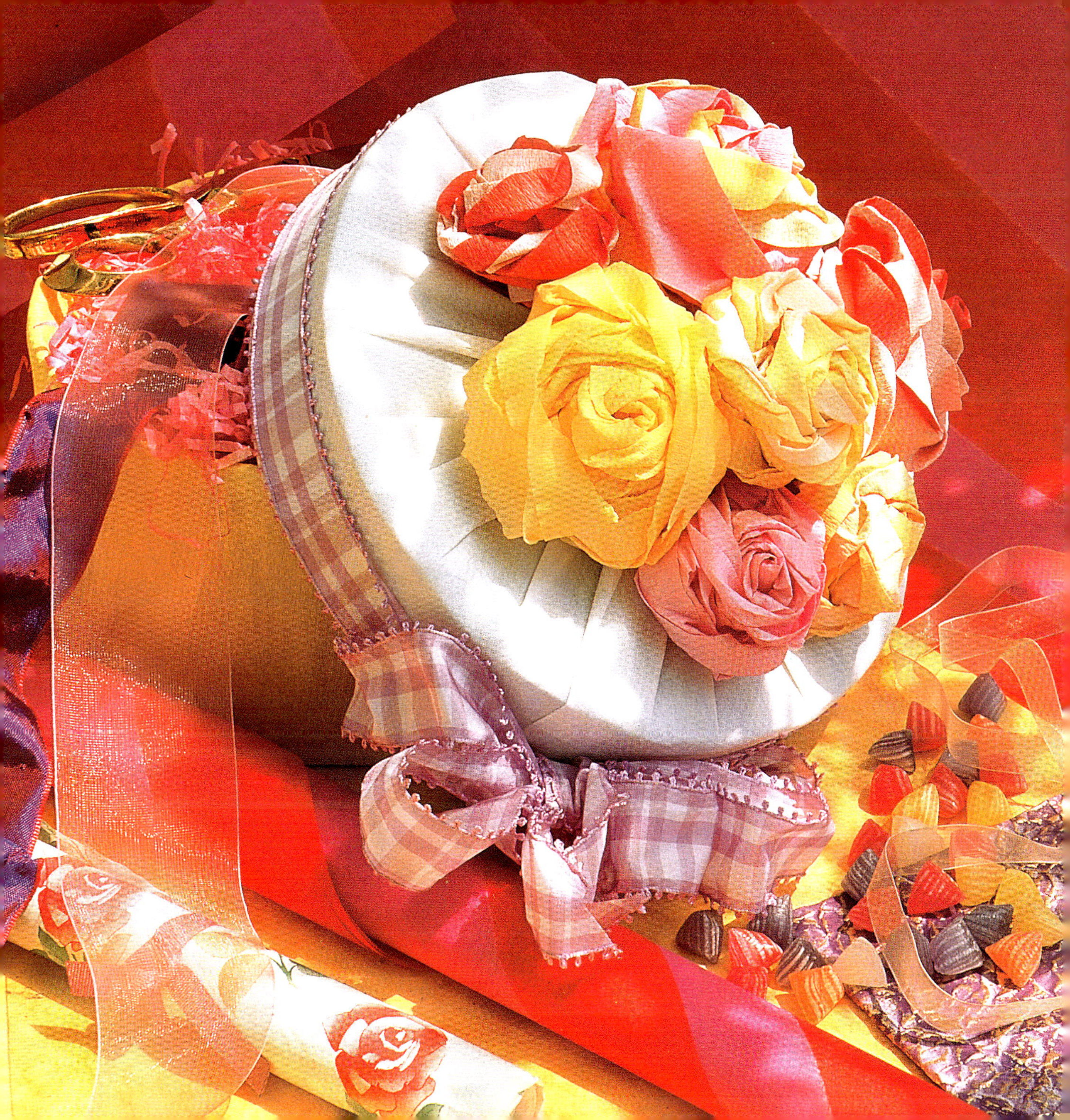

ROSE APPLIQUE BAG

This attractive shopping bag recycles old table linen, fabric remnants and buttons. Look for unworn areas of old tablecloths or damask napkins; even the smallest scraps can combine effectively with other kinds of material.

YOU WILL NEED

MATERIALS
rose-print furnishing fabric
  remnant
fusible bonding web
striped or checked table napkins,
  cloths or remnants
calico, 24 x 33 inches
matching sewing thread
6 old buttons

EQUIPMENT
dressmaking scissors
iron
tracing paper
pencil
sewing machine
vanishing fabric marker
ruler
safety pin
needle

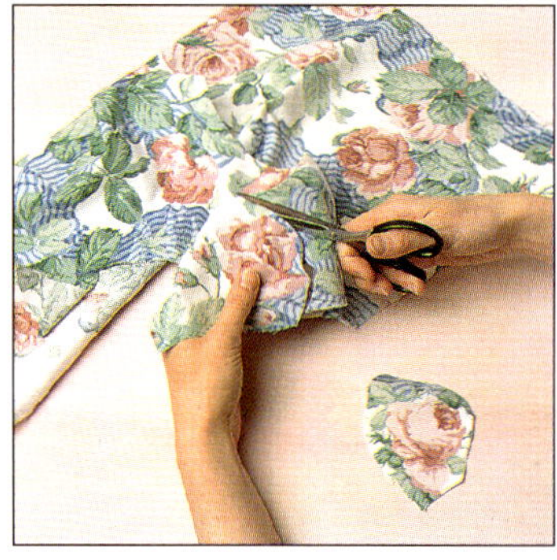

1 Pick out five interesting rose motifs and eight single leaf motifs from the fabric and cut them out roughly.

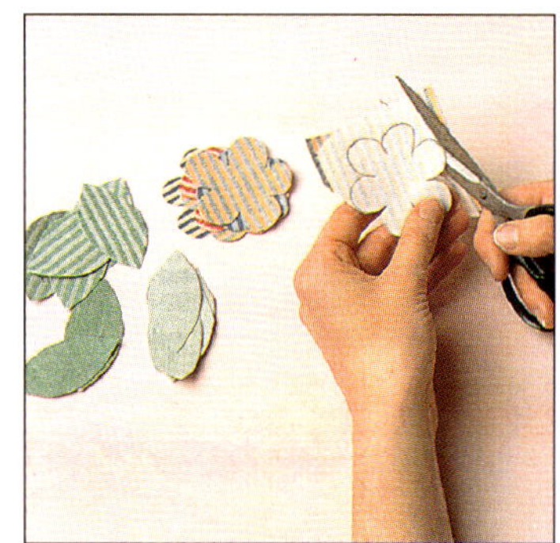

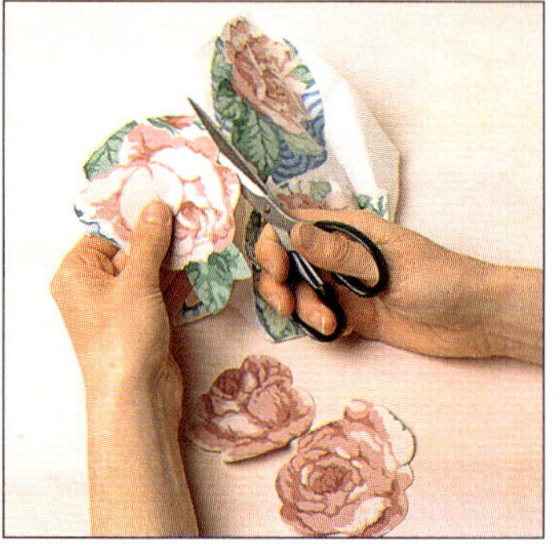

2 Iron the wrong side of the roses and leaves to the bonding web. Cut around the edges, simplifying the outlines to make them easier to sew.

3 Enlarge the templates from the back of the book as necessary and trace six flower shapes onto the paper side of more bonding web. Cut them out roughly and iron them onto the striped or checked fabrics. Cut around the outlines. Make ten leaves in the same way and one large blue and white jug.

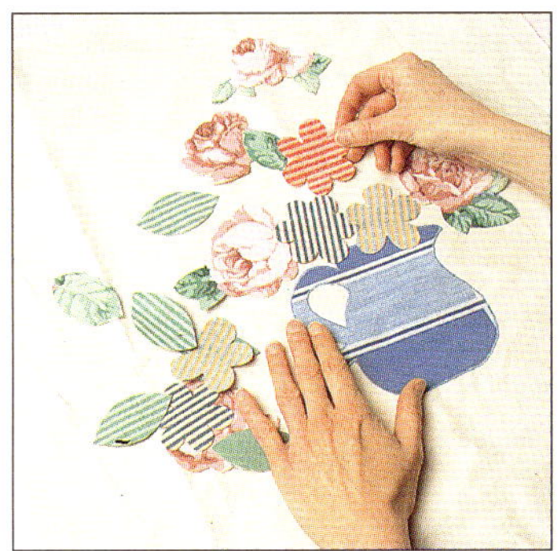

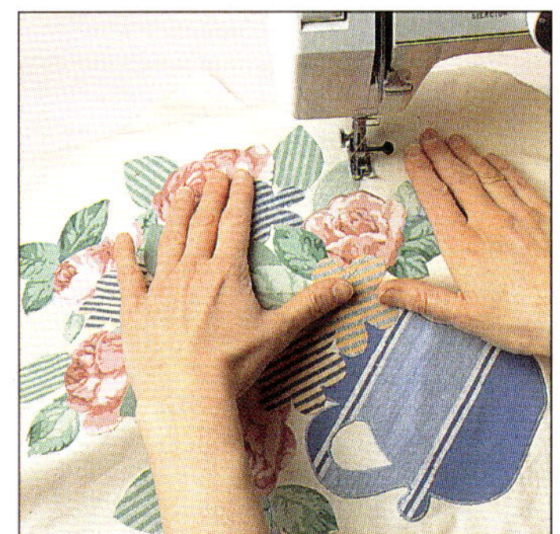

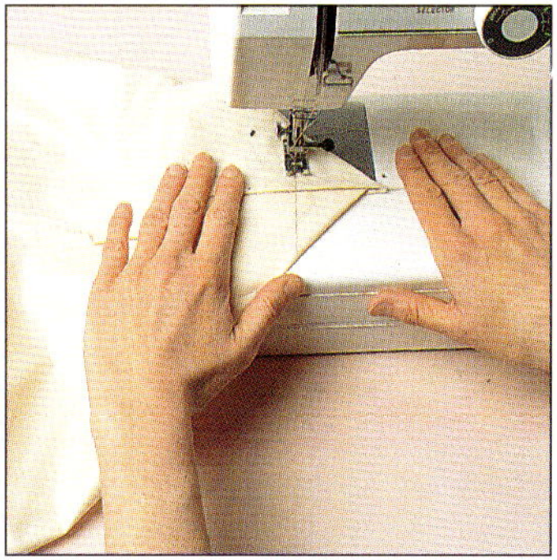

4 Cut a 20 x 33-inch calico rectangle and fold it in half crosswise. Peel the backing paper from the pitcher and iron in place on the center front. Using matching thread and a narrow satin stitch, sew in place. Remove the backing paper from the leaves and flowers and arrange them around the jug. Iron in place.

5 Sew the shapes in place with the satin stitch, using matching thread and working over the outside edges of the fabric. Finish off all the threads on the wrong side.

6 Attach the bottom and side edges with French seams, for strength. Turn inside out and flatten one corner, to make a right-angled point at the end of the bottom seam. Measure 2 inches down from the end and mark a line across the corner. Sew across this line. Repeat for the other corner, to make a flat base for the bag.

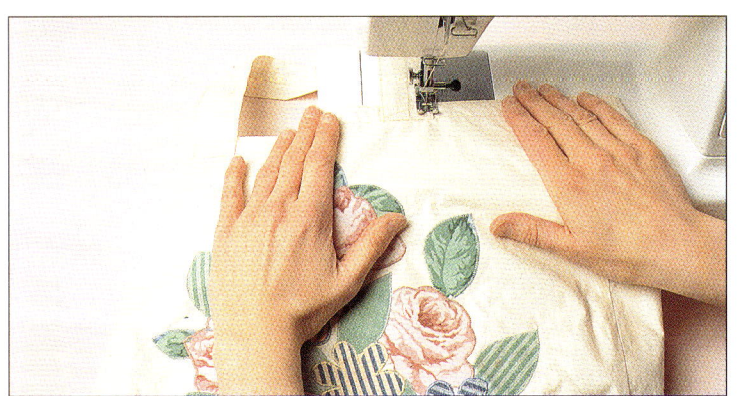

7 Turn under, press and stitch a double hem of 1 inch around the top of the bag. Cut the remaining calico into two equal strips and fold each in half lengthwise. Attach 1 inch from the outside edge and, using a safety pin, turn inside out. Top-stitch both sides and sew one handle to each side of the bag.

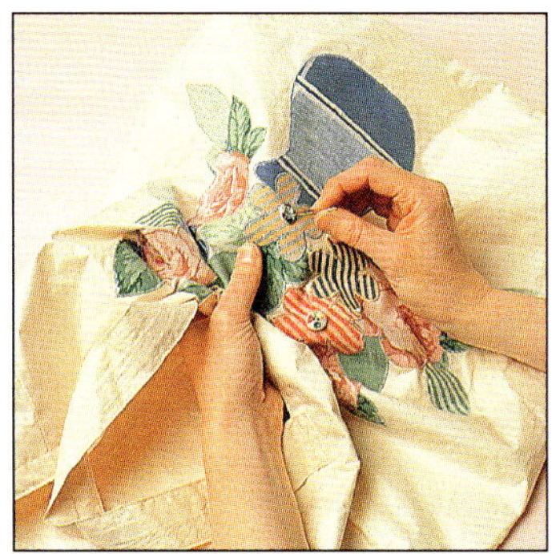

8 Sew a button to the center of each plain flower, as a finishing touch.

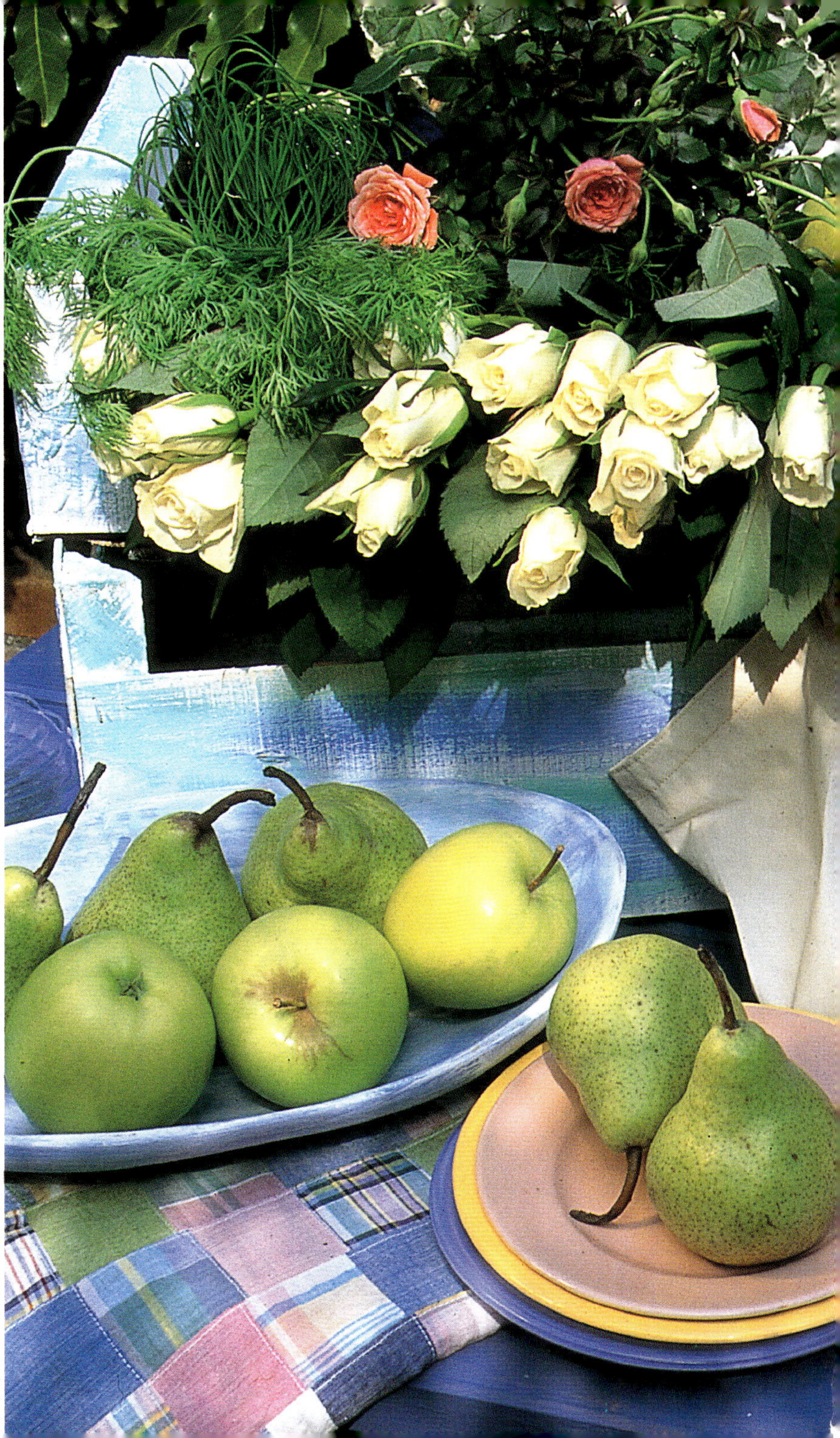

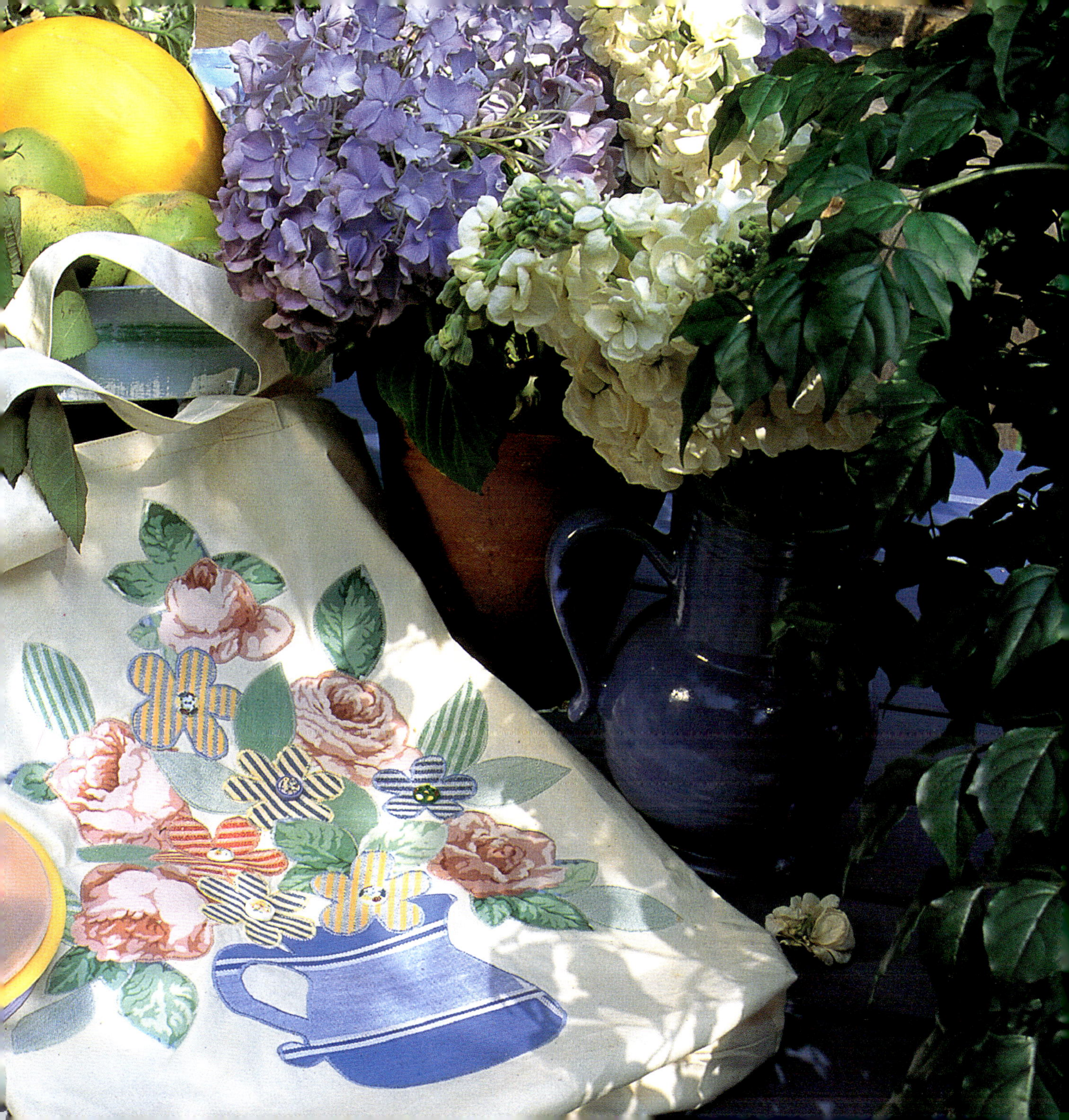

YELLOW ROSES LAMPSHADE

A hand-decorated lamp-shade makes the perfect finishing touch to a room-scheme. This particularly charming one has roses made from textured paper that are enhanced when the light is switched on.

MATERIALS
yellow and green textured paper
  fabric lampshade
white glue
matte water-based acrylic
varnish

EQUIPMENT
tracing paper
soft pencil
paper
fine black felt-tipped pen
sharp pencil
scissors
paintbrush

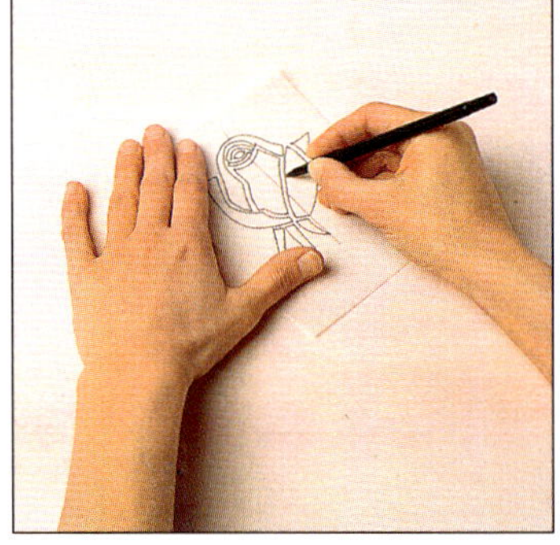

1 Trace and enlarge the rose templates from the back of the book. Go over the lines again with the black pen.

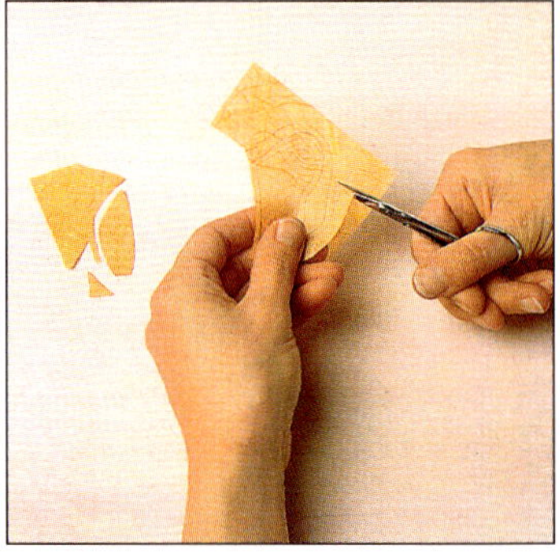

2 Lay the yellow paper over the motif and trace the outline showing through, using a sharp pencil. Cut carefully along the lines and lay the pieces out on a flat surface. Trace and cut out the green pieces in the same way.

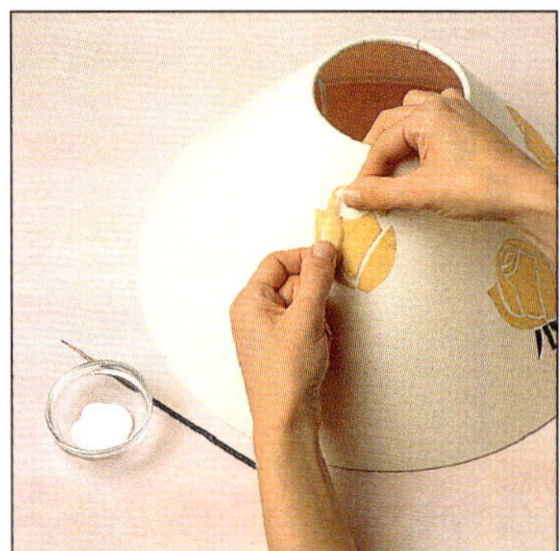

3 Stick the shapes onto the shade, spreading a thin layer of glue on the reverse of each piece as you go. Using the traced rose as a guide, stagger the motifs over the lampshade.

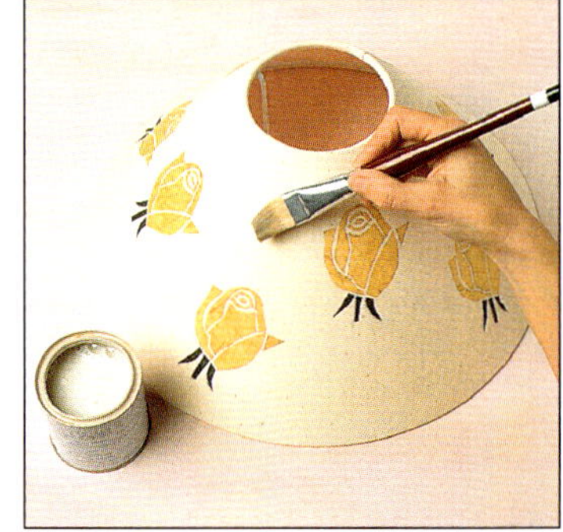

4 Glue the calyx and stem under each rose. Once the glue has dried, paint the shade with two coats of varnish.

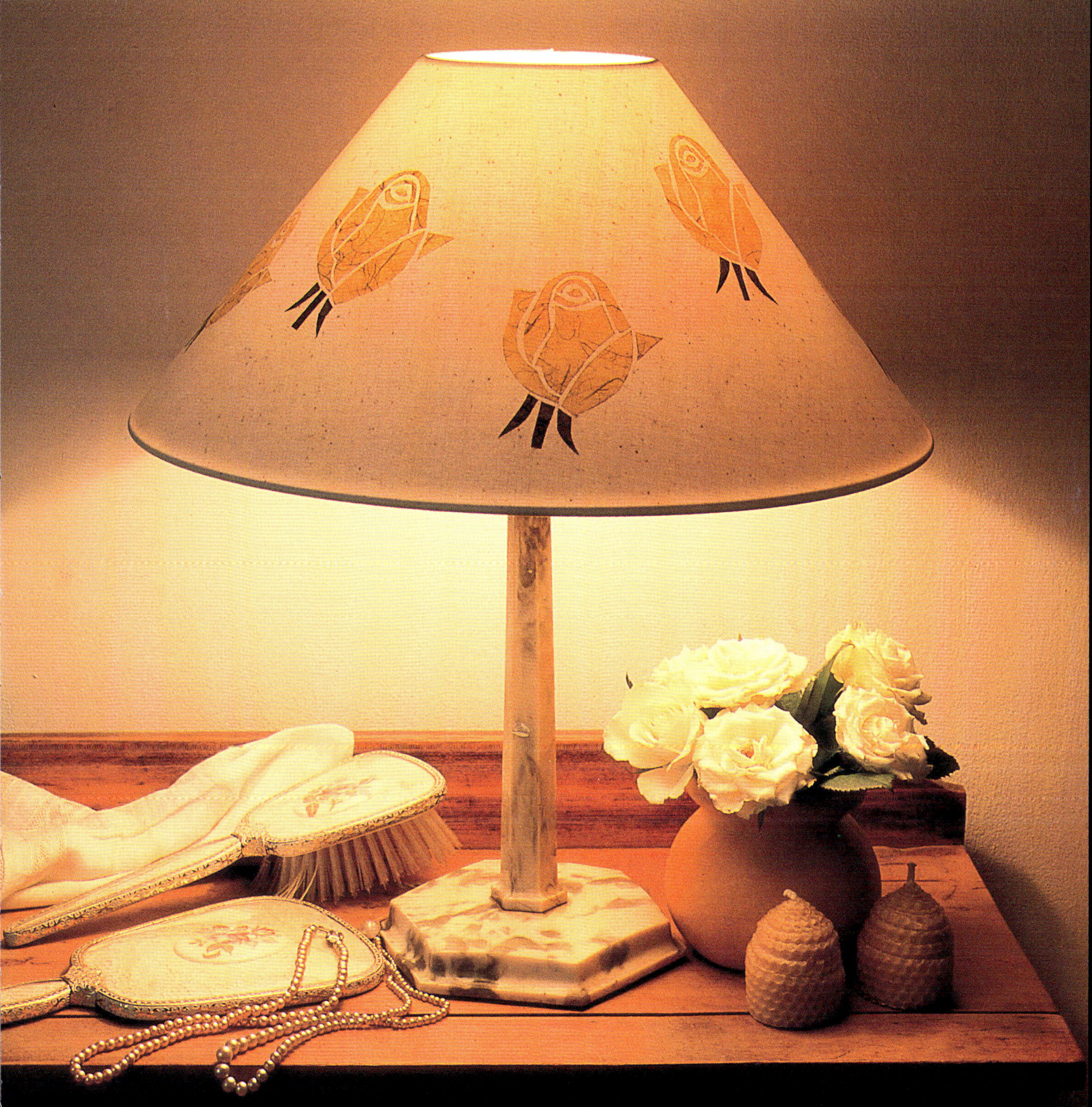

R O S E B U D - P A I N T E D   P I T C H E R

Transform a plain glass pitcher with your own, individual design. If you are a beginner at painting on glass, you might find it easier to trace the template from the back of the book onto paper and fit the paper inside the pitcher. Then trace the design with the outliner. This helps you to space the design evenly around the jug, so you do not run out of space.

YOU WILL NEED

MATERIALS
glass pitcher
hot soapy water
gold glass-painting outliner
  tubing
glass paint: red and green

EQUIPMENT
alcohol
paper towels
bubble wrap or bag of lentils
paintbrush
turpentine

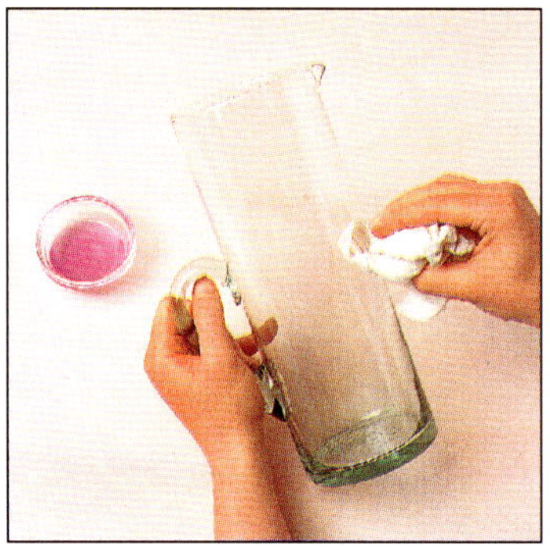

1 Wash the pitcher in hot soapy water and dry it thoroughly. Wipe it with alcohol on paper towels, to remove any traces of grease.

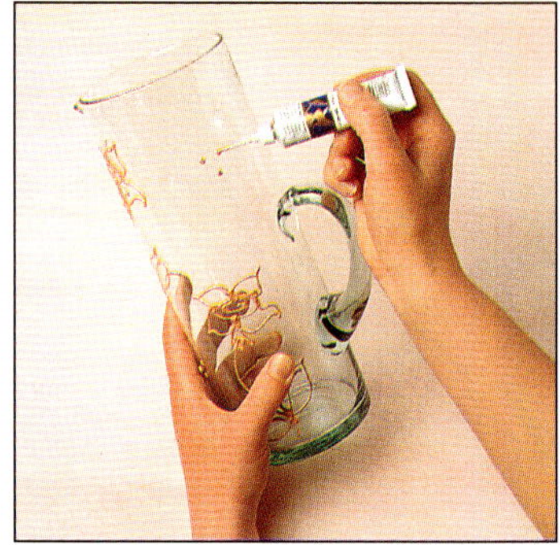

2 Controlling the flow of the outliner tubing can be tricky, so make a few practice runs on an old jam jar. Once you are feeling confident, draw your design on the pitcher. This is easiest to do in sections; each section should be left for at least 12 hours, to harden, before you begin the next.

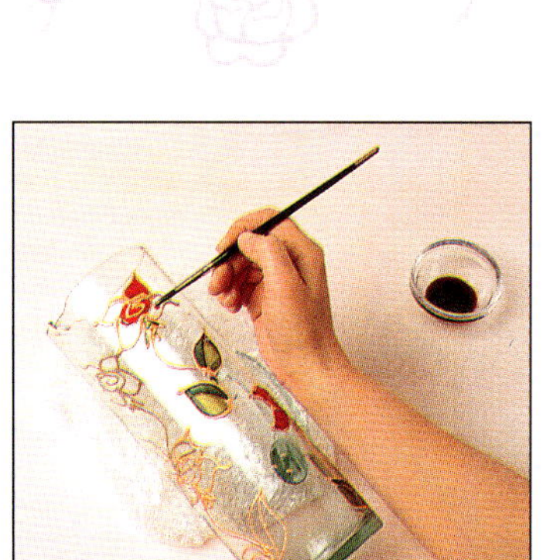

3 To fill in the design, prop the pitcher up on its side on the bubble wrap. Try to keep the area that you are painting horizontal, to stop the paint from running. Carefully paint in a section, applying the paint thickly, to prevent streaky brush strokes. Remove excess paint with the brush. Let each section dry overnight before turning the pitcher to do the next section. Clean the brush with turpentine each time.

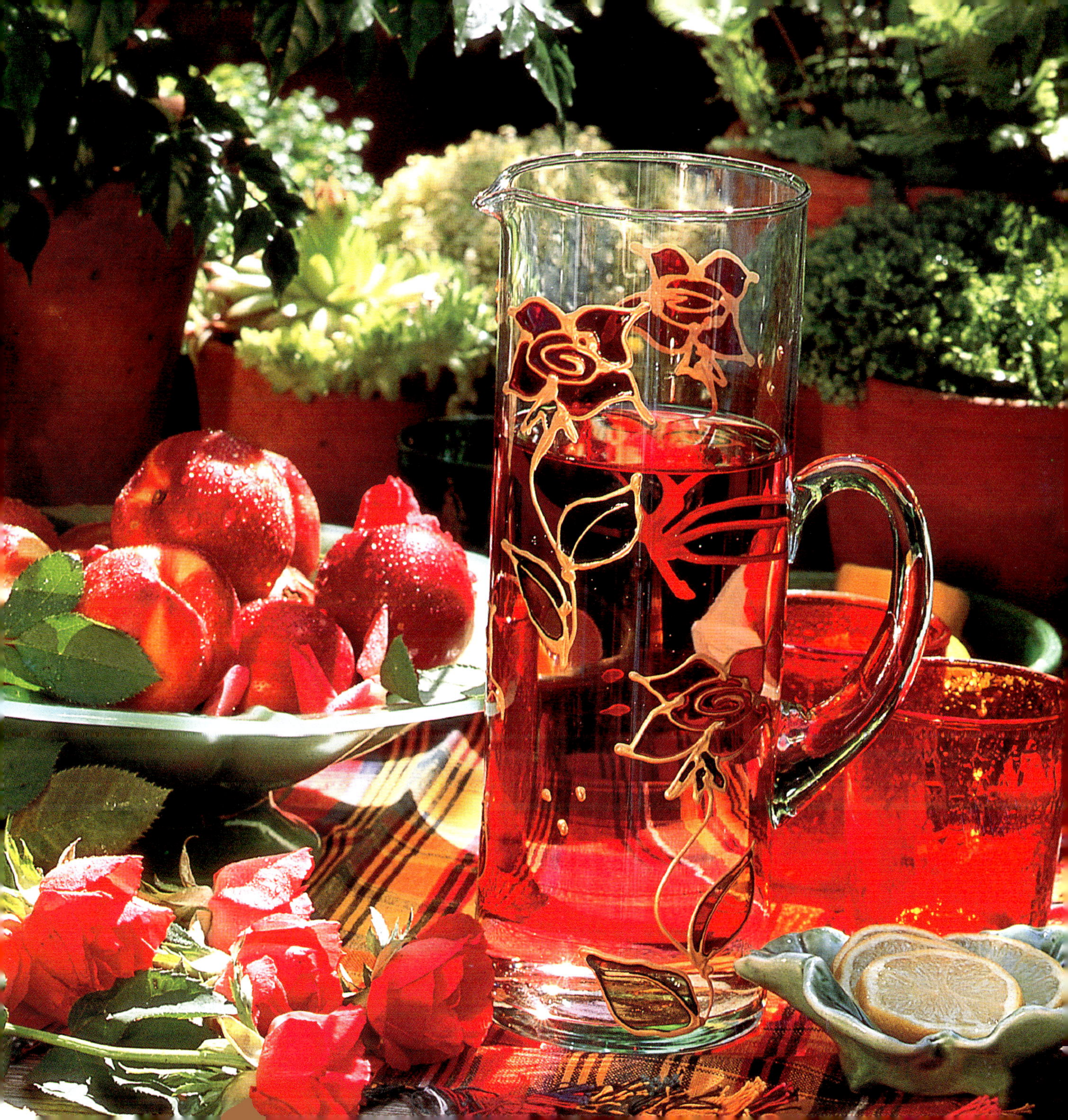

D E C O U P A G E R O S E E G G S

R euse salvaged wrapping paper or look out for reproductions of brightly printed Victorian scrapbook rose motifs to make these densely patterned eggs.

You Will Need

Materials
*rose scrapbook motifs or rose-
  decorated wrapping paper
white glue
wooden or blown eggs
clear nail polish*

Equipment
*small sharp scissors
paintbrush*

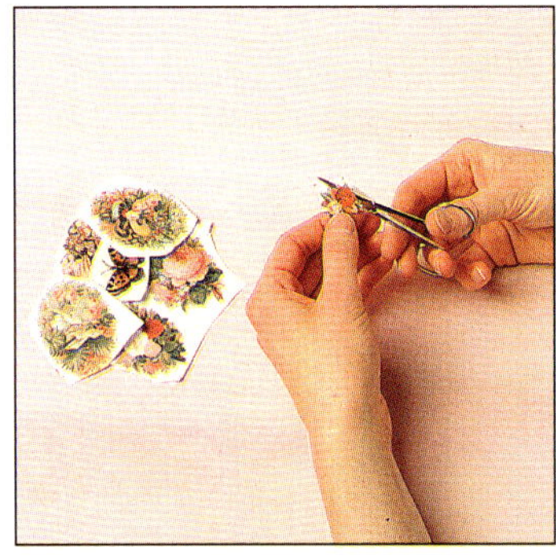

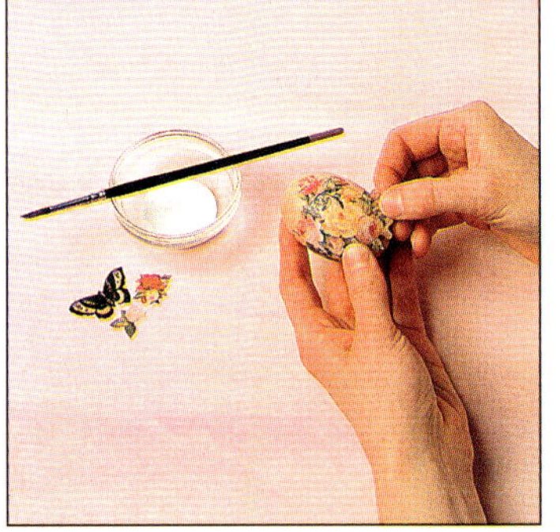

1 Cut out a selection of small rose motifs. You may find other motifs you can incorporate, such as butterflies or forget-me-nots. Look for interesting shapes and cut carefully around the outlines.

2 Using white glue, stick the cut-out flowers to the eggs, overlapping the edges to make a densely patterned surface. Make sure that all the wood or shell is covered.

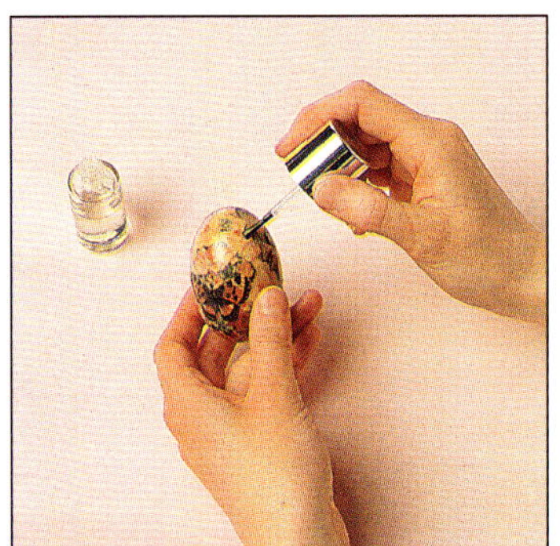

3 When the glue is dry, coat the eggs with three or four coats of clear nail polish, allowing each coat to dry completely before adding the next.

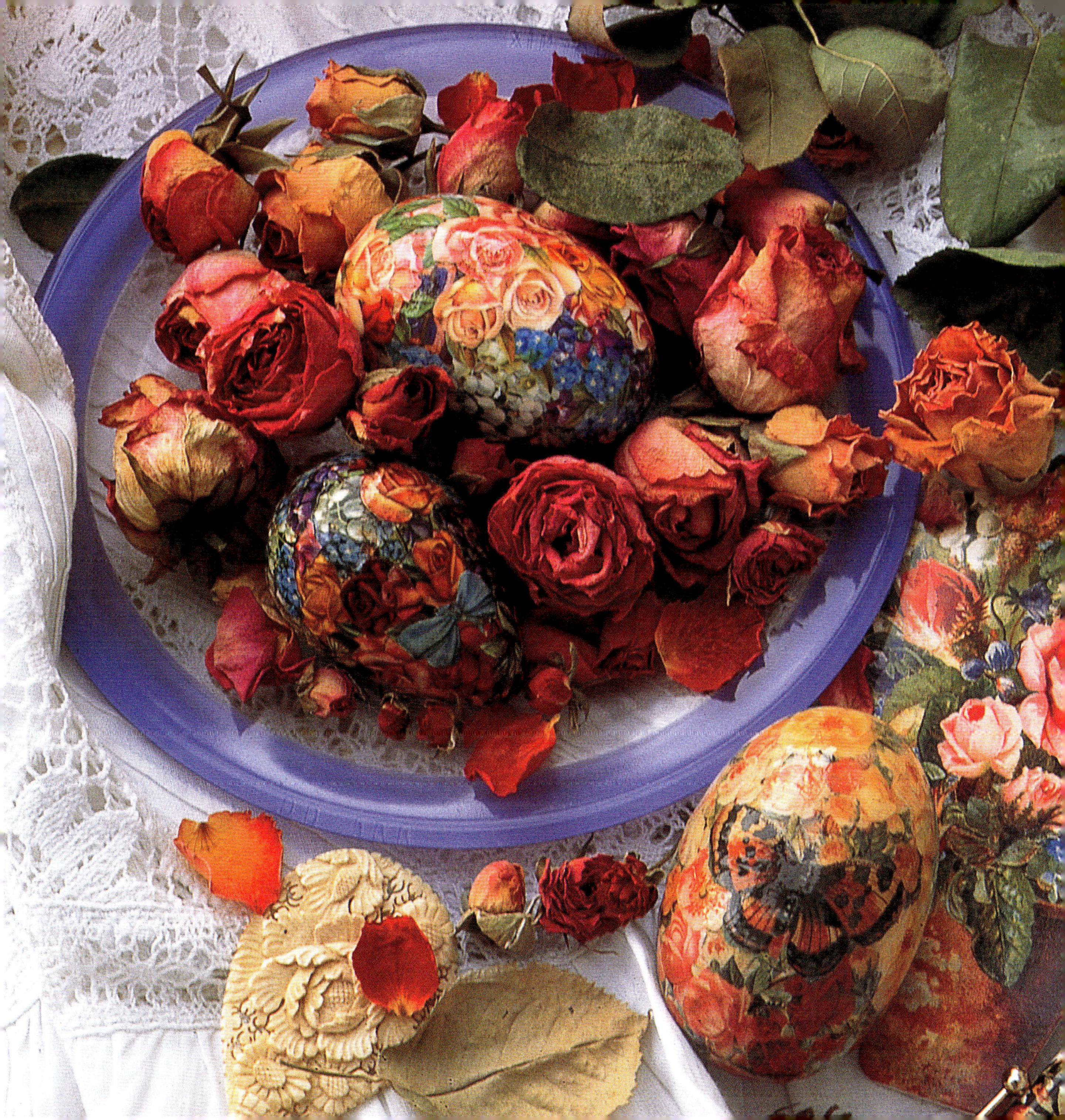

SATIN ROSE HAT DECORATION

Decorate a straw hat for a summer wedding or garden party with a vibrant rose made of satin ribbon. Combine ribbons of different widths and colors to make a bunch of roses, or stick to one beautiful specimen that will catch every eye.

YOU WILL NEED

MATERIALS
*satin ribbons in
  3 complementary shades
matching sewing thread
28-gauge green florist's stem
  wires
green ribbon
green crêpe paper or florist's
  tape*

EQUIPMENT
*scissors
needle*

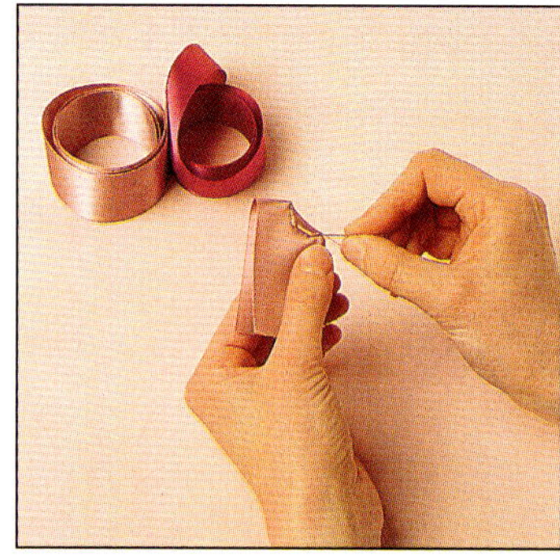

1 Make each petal separately, starting with the center petal. Cut a piece of ribbon, about twice the width of the ribbon in length, and fold it with wrong sides together. Fold over each of the top corners twice and stitch them down invisibly. Repeat to make enough petals for a rose, using different shades and widths of ribbon.

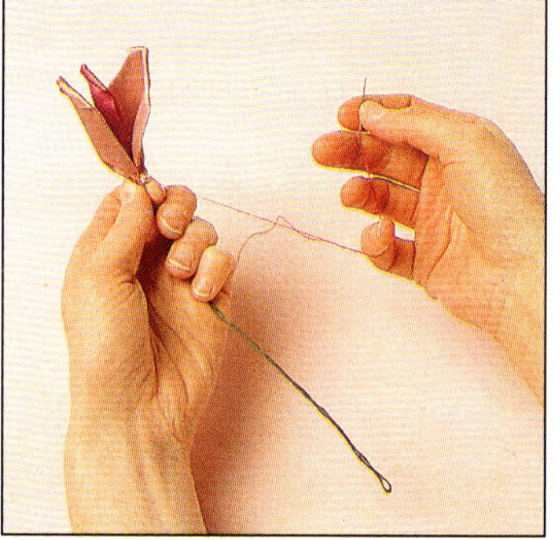

2 Roll the center petal around itself and secure with a stitch. Insert a stem wire into this first petal and continue to add petals around the rose, stitching them together as you go.

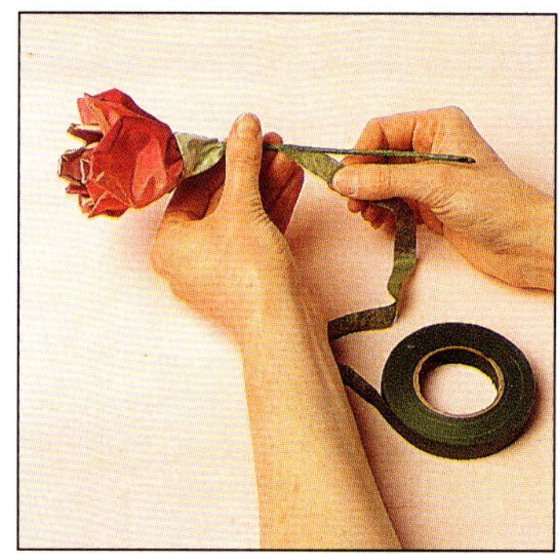

3 Finish the rose by binding with green ribbon, to hide the raw edges. Stitch it in place at the top, just over the base of the petals, and then gather up the lower edge neatly and stitch it to secure. Bind the stem with crêpe paper or florist's tape.

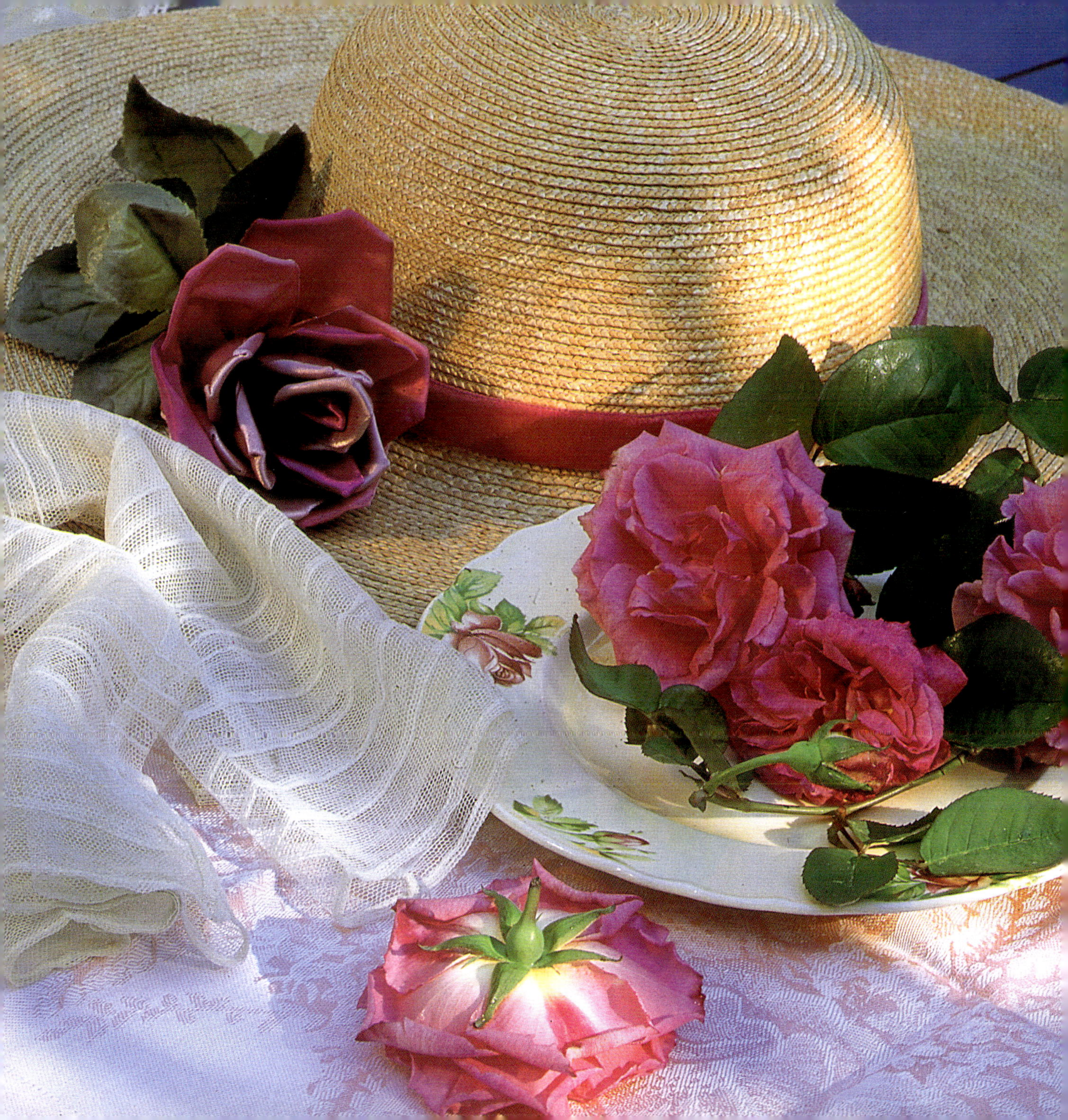

VELVET ROSE COAT HANGER

Perfect for hanging up a special garment or to give as a gift, this coat hanger makes use of the luxurious texture and rich colors of velvet to re-create the charm of roses in full bloom. Ready-made fabric leaves are widely available.

YOU WILL NEED

MATERIALS
batting
wooden clothes hanger
matching sewing threads
green and red velvet
fabric leaves
matching narrow velvet ribbon

EQUIPMENT
dressmaking scissors
tape measure
needle
paper
pencil
sewing machine

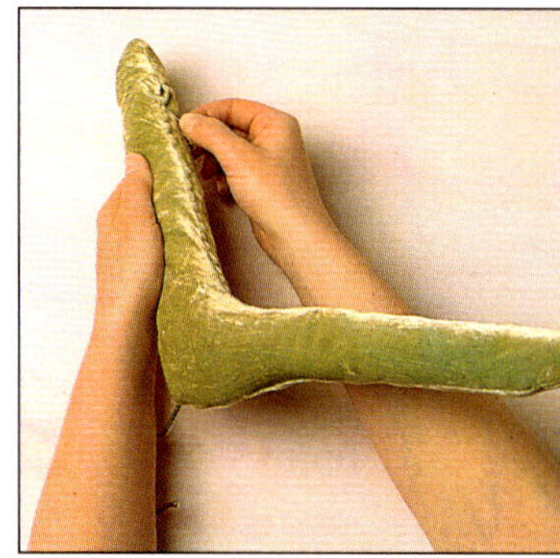

1 Cut two pieces of batting about 12 inches square. Wrap each arm of the hanger in batting and sew it in place. To make a paper template, put the hanger on a sheet of paper and draw around it. Add ⅜ inch all around, and around the ends. Cut two pieces of green velvet to this size. With right sides together, stitch the upper edge and the rounded ends. Turn right sides out. Unpick the center and slip the velvet over the hanger. Slip-stitch the bottom edges together.

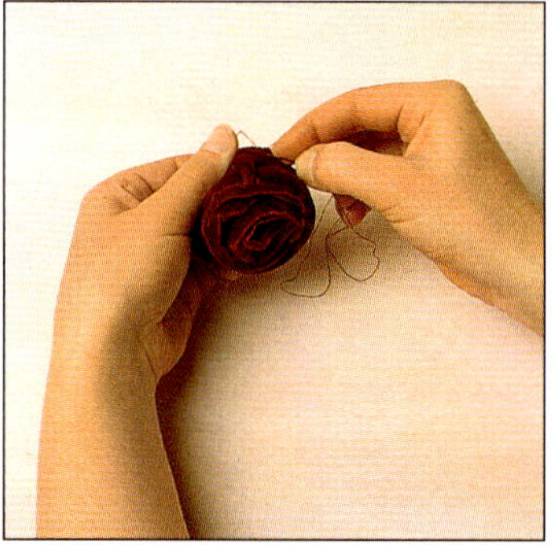

2 Cut a piece of red velvet 4 x 12 inches, fold it in half lengthwise and stitch the long edge and one short edge. Turn right sides out. Roll up the velvet from the unstitched short end to make a rose, and secure it with a prick stitch.

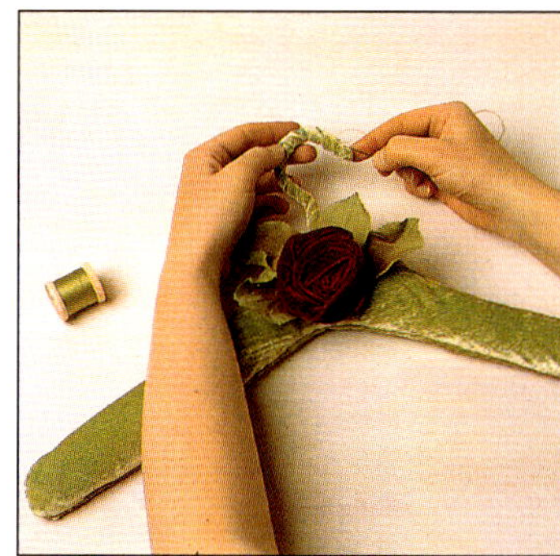

3 Stitch the rose and fabric leaves to the center of the hanger. Wrap the ribbon round the hook and slip-stitch.

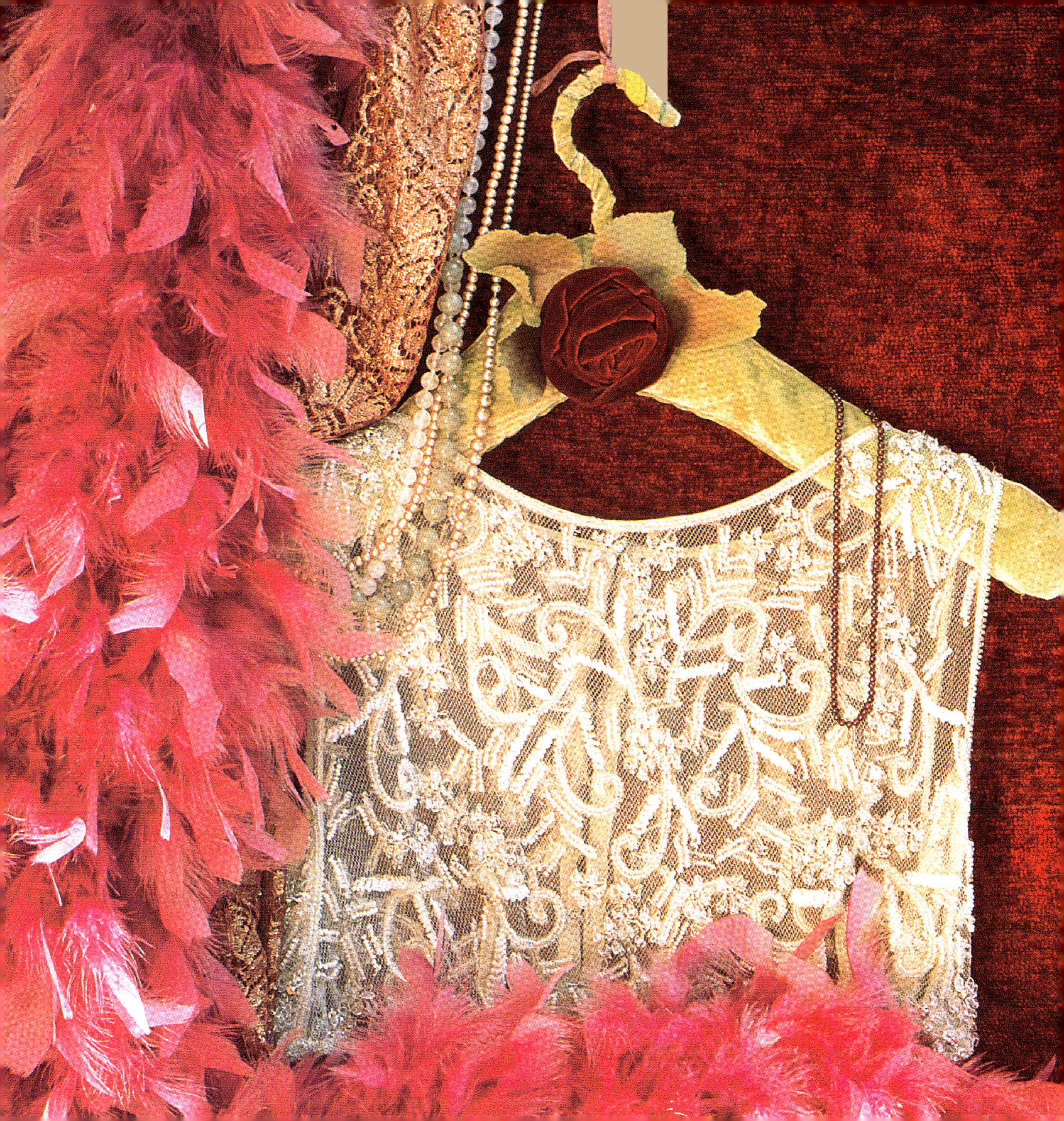

WILD ROSE CHIFFON SCARF

Shimmering silk chiffon or organza and glittering silver metallic paint combine here to make a ravishing scarf that would completely transform a plain outfit. You do not have to wear this, though; it is a technique that could equally well be used to make beautiful fabric wall hangings.

YOU WILL NEED

MATERIALS
silk chiffon or organza,
  12 x 20 inches
silver metallic fabric paint
metallic paint with nozzle-tipped
  dispenser

EQUIPMENT
iron
wooden frame
drawing pins
tracing paper
pencil
paintbrush
vanishing fabric marker
needle

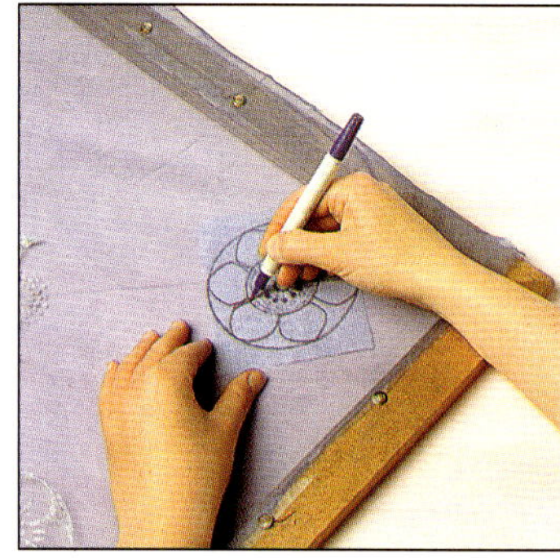

1 Wash, dry and iron the silk. Fold in half and press twice. Fold diagonally and press. Unfold and stretch the fabric taut on the frame, using drawing pins. Make sure the fabric is straight. Enlarge the template at the back of the book. Trace the motif onto the back of the silk in the center. Trace eight more motifs around it, using the folds as a guide.

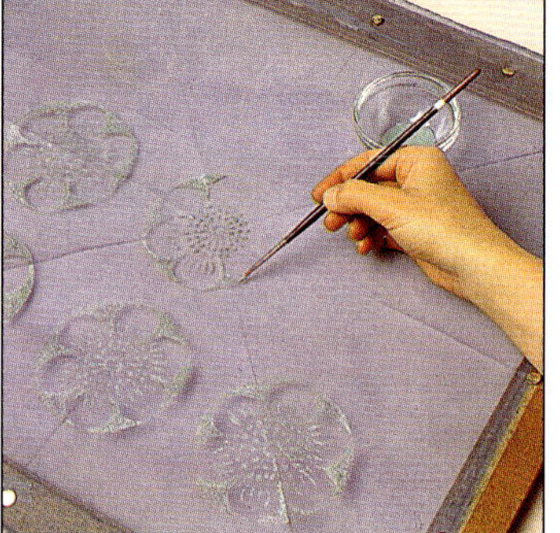

2 Turn the frame over and go over the outlines of the design with silver paint on the front of the fabric. Let dry. Unpin the scarf and iron it, to set the paint, following the manufacturer's instructions. Stretch the fabric again.

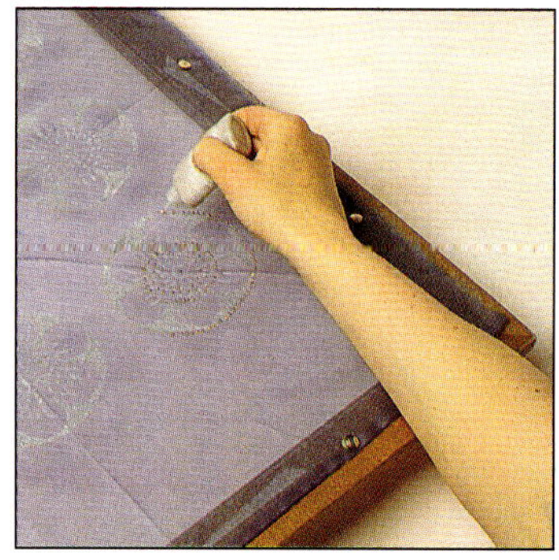

3 Using the nozzle-tipped tube, make dots of metallic paint around the outer edges of each rose and fill in the details. Mark lines of dots 2 inches from the edges of the scarf, with the marker. To fray the edges, work one side at a time. Use a needle to separate and remove threads from the raw edges, then pull away up to the dotted edges.

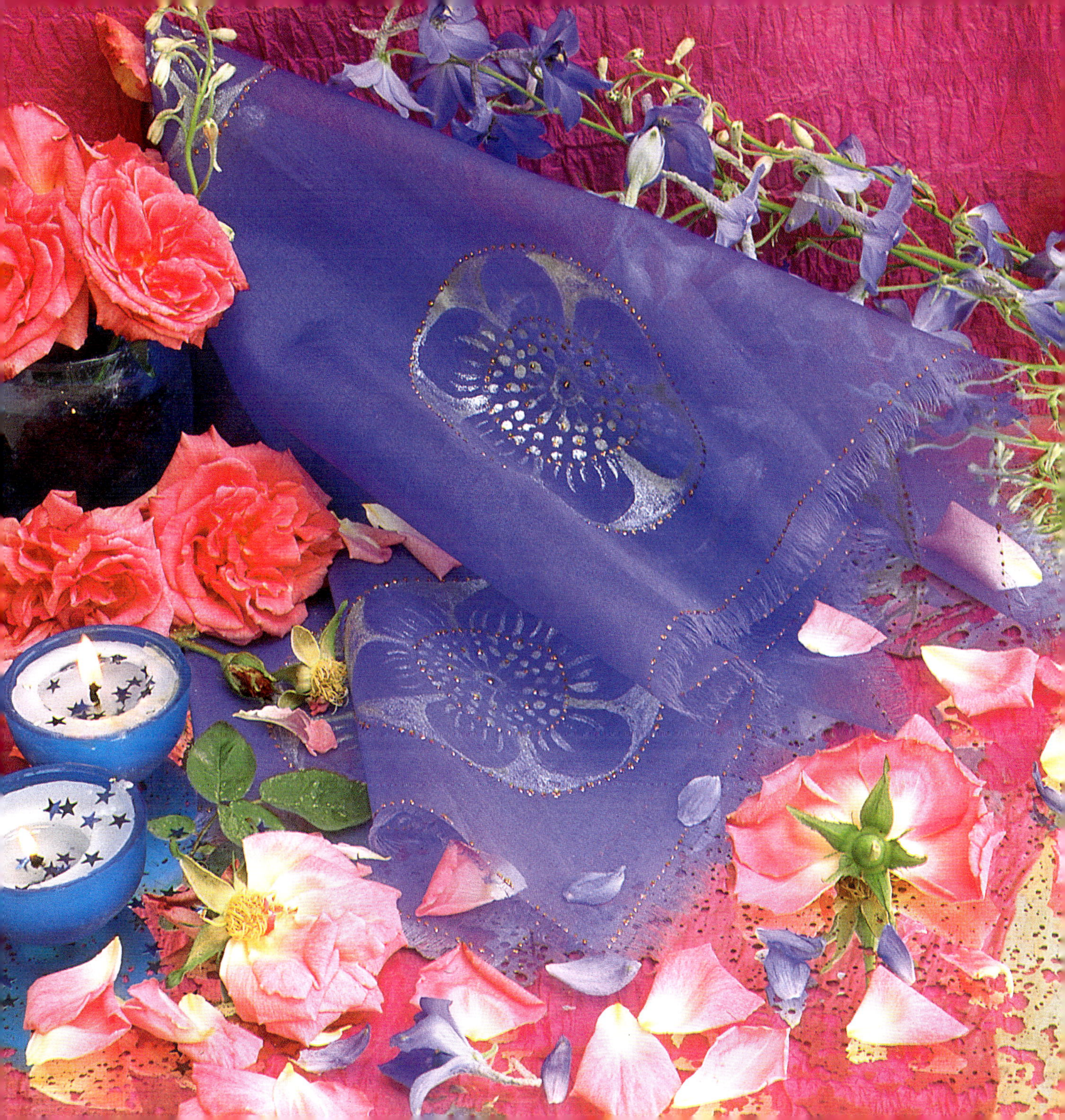

ROSE PATCHWORK THROW

This patchwork throw is an ideal way to use up odd remnants of furnishing fabrics. Your local upholsterer may sell old sample books, which are a good source of different rose prints and contrasting weaves.

YOU WILL NEED

MATERIALS
selection of rose-printed and plain fabrics
matching sewing thread
dusky red heavyweight Jacquard-weave fabric, 4 feet 7 inches square, for backing
25 small buttons
woven furnishing braid, 5 yards, 7 inches

EQUIPMENT
iron
dressmaking scissors
rotary cutter
quilter's square rule
cutting mat
sewing machine
dressmaker's pins and basting thread, or safety pins
needle

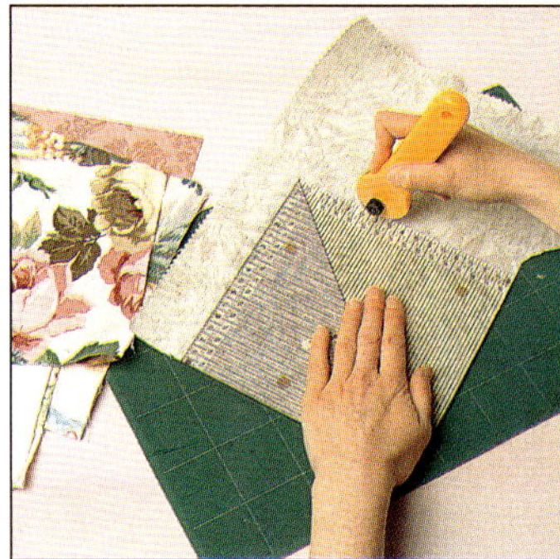

1 Iron the fabrics and cut out 18 plain and 18 patterned squares, each 8 inches square. For accuracy, use a rotary cutter and quilter's square for this, or make a paper template as a guide.

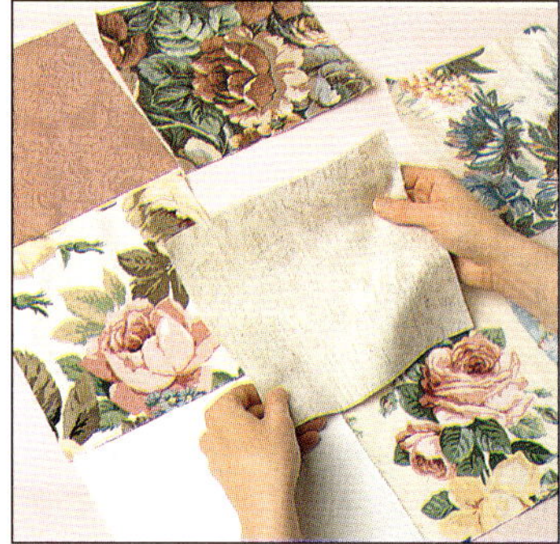

2 Lay the pieces on the floor to form a checkerboard of alternate plain and printed squares. Take the time to find a pleasing balance of colors.

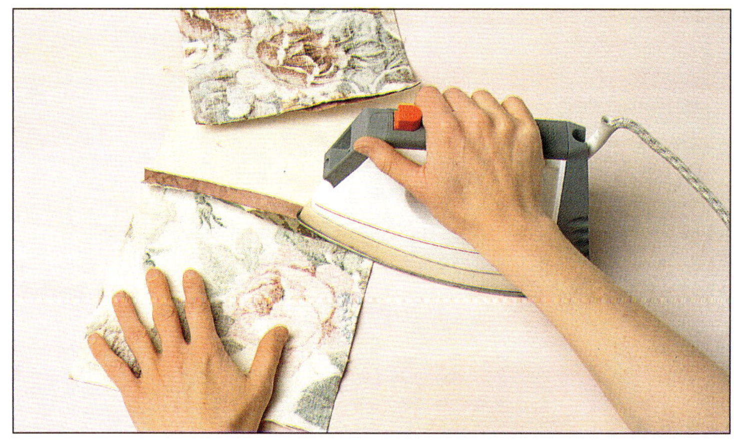

3 Sew rows of three squares together, leaving seam allowances of ½ inch. Press the seams open.

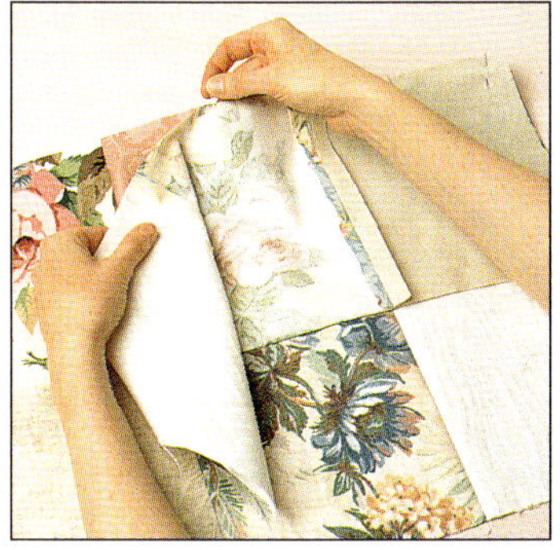

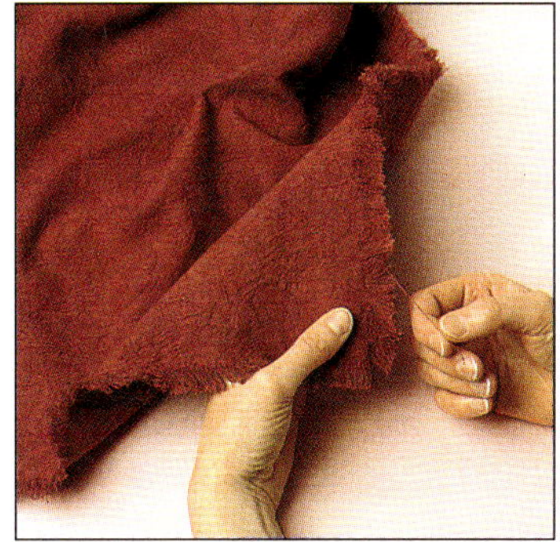

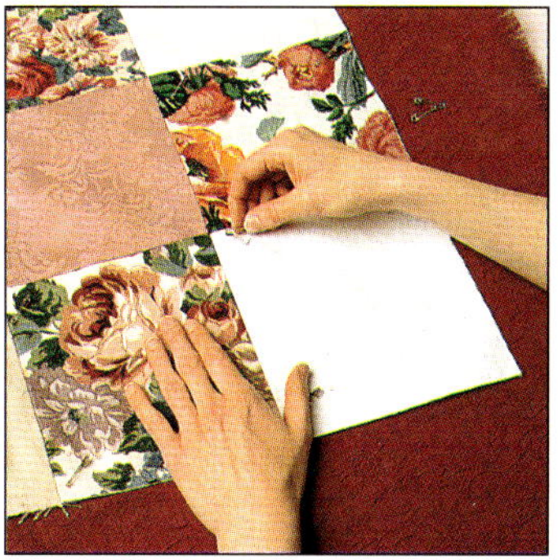

4 Sew three rows together, with the same seam allowances, carefully matching the seams to assemble four blocks of 3 x 3 squares. Sew the four blocks together, to form one large square.

5 Square up the edges of the backing fabric. Fringe the edges by pulling away threads from each side.

6 Place the patchwork square in the center of the backing fabric. Pin and baste or safety pin it in place.

7 Sew the patchwork in place, by firmly attaching a button at each intersection point. Be sure to sew through all the layers of fabric.

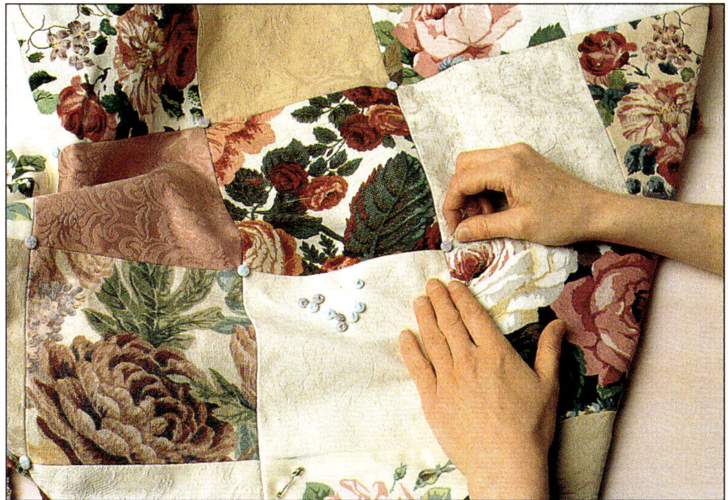

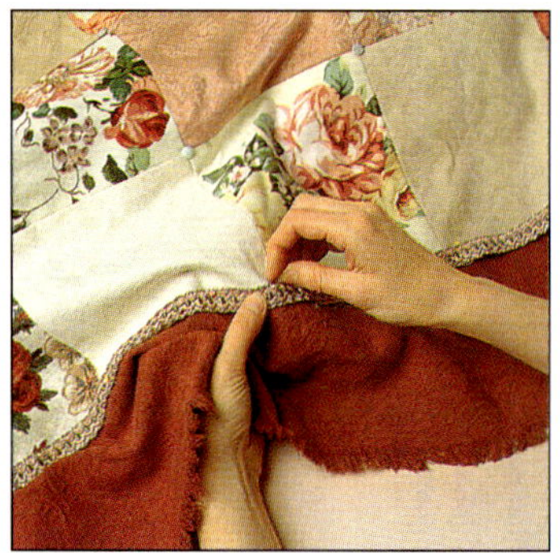

8 Slip-stitch the braid onto the backing to attach and conceal the raw edges, mitering the corners as you sew.

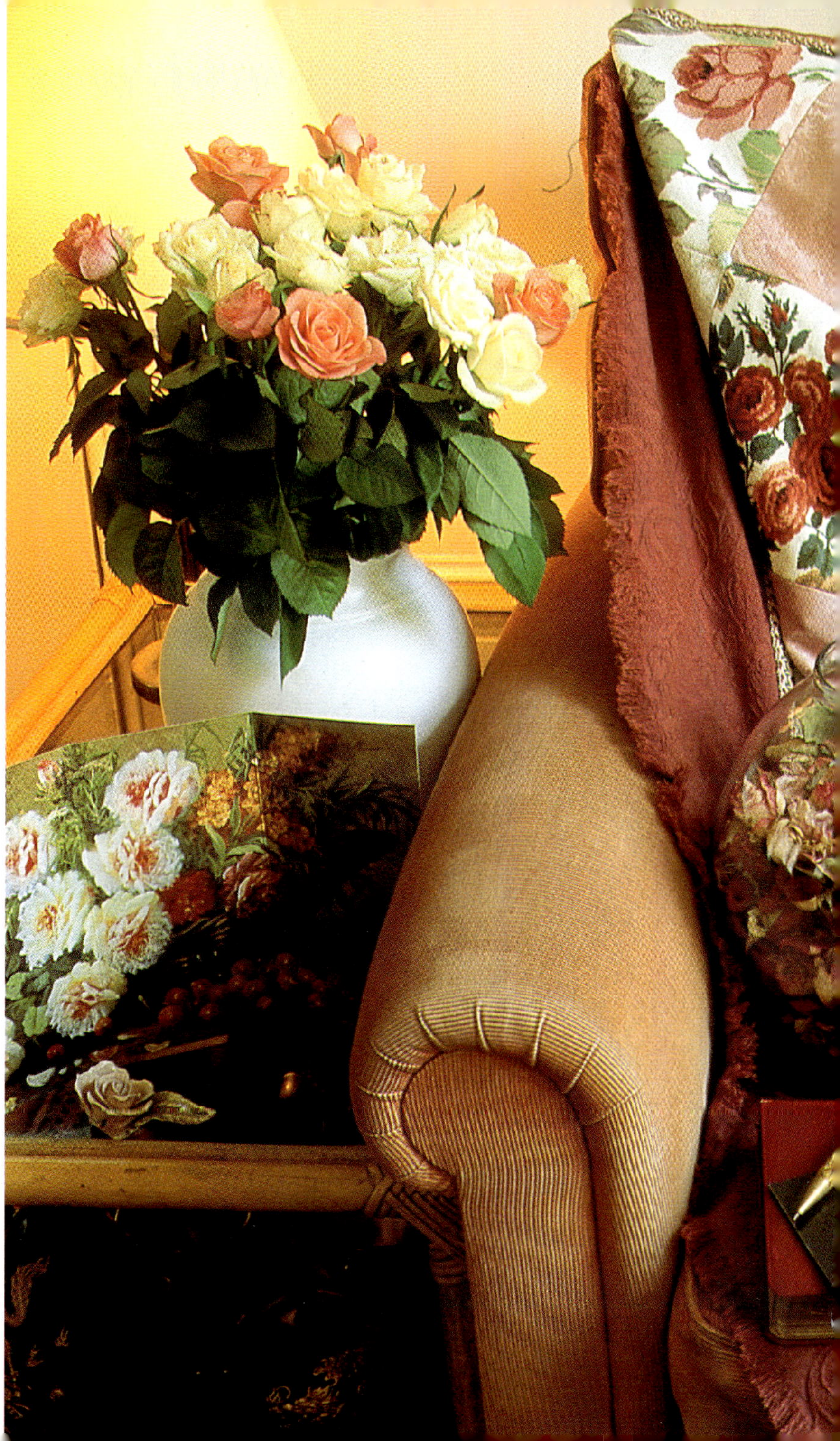

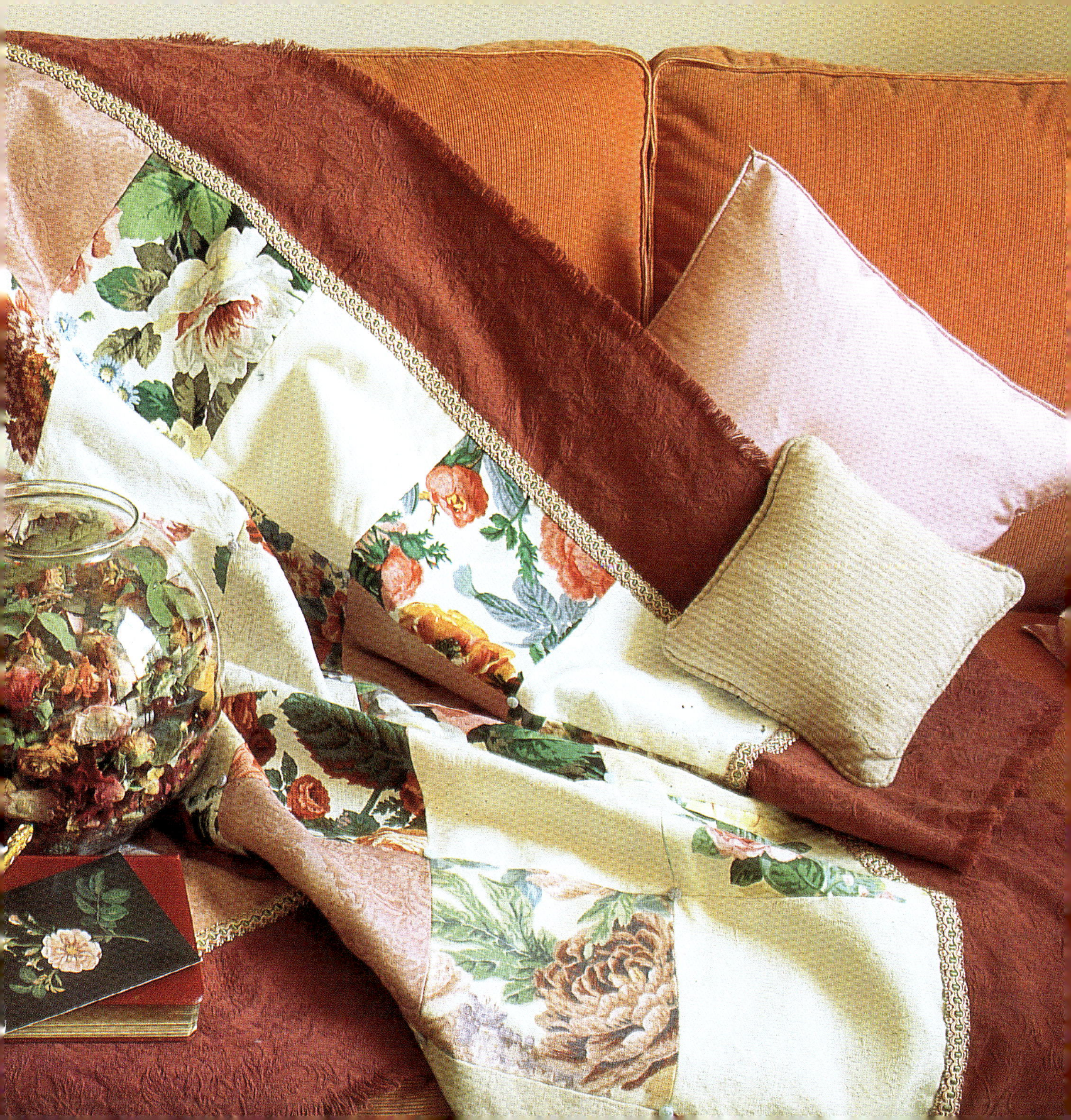

MINIATURE ROSE BROOCH

Polymer clay is a marvelous medium for molding. It is much easier to use than clay and can be baked hard in an ordinary oven. The colors are jewel-like in their intensity and yet this hand-made brooch has a charming simplicity, reminiscent of folk art.

YOU WILL NEED

MATERIALS
*polymer clay: carmine, green
  and golden yellow*
earring posts
epoxy resin glue
brooch pin

EQUIPMENT
rose nail
aluminum foil
small rolling pin
kitchen knife
clover-shaped cookie cutter

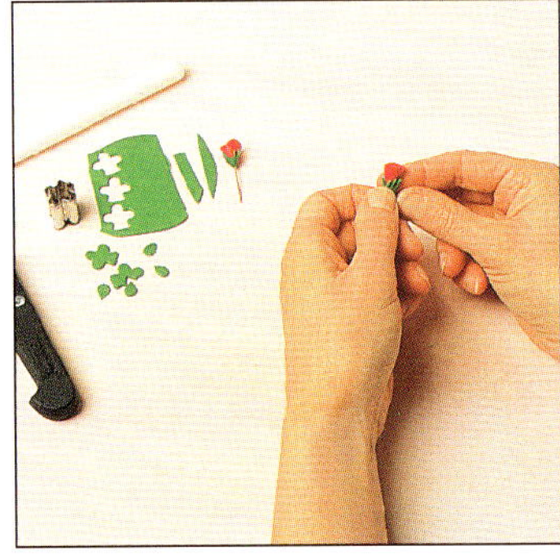

1 Roll three small balls of carmine clay for each rose. Flatten a ball between your finger and thumb and wrap around the rose nail. Overlap the petals as you work and gently open out the bud with your finger. Ease off the nail and insert an earring post. Push into a ball of foil.

Make another four roses in the same way. Bake at 225°F for 10–15 minutes. Roll out the green clay thinly. With a kitchen knife, cut small squares and fringe one edge. Wrap this around the base of the rose to form the calyx. Cut out several clover shapes, using the cutter. Cut three leaves from each and mark veins with the knife.

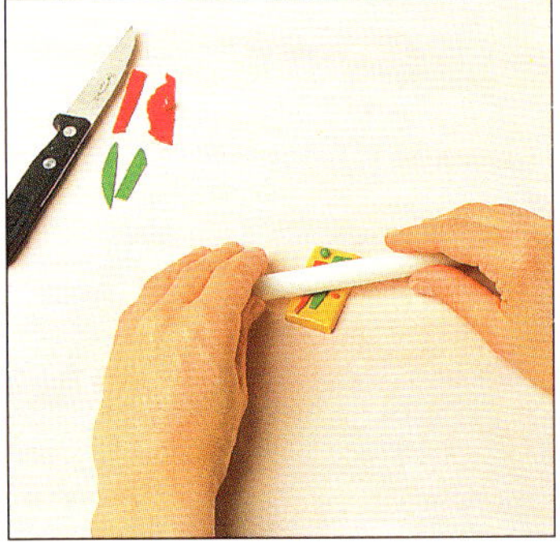

2 Roll out a ¾ x 2-inch rectangle of yellow clay for the vase. Lay thin pieces of carmine and green clay on top as decoration. Roll the pieces flat and mark with a knife.

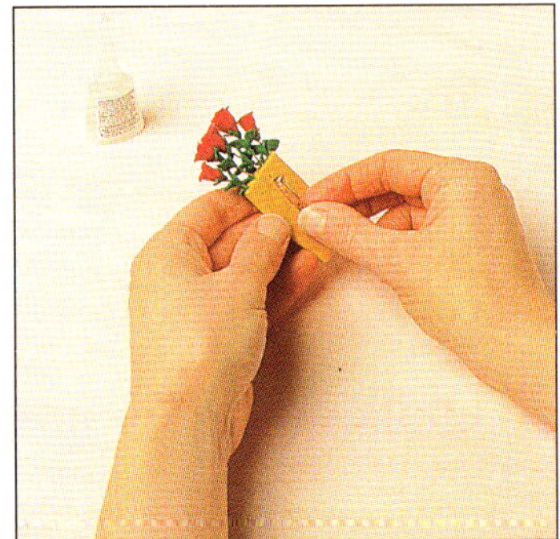

3 Press leaves around the roses, and put them in the vase. Put leaves on the edge. Bake at 225°F for 30 minutes. When cool, glue on the pin.

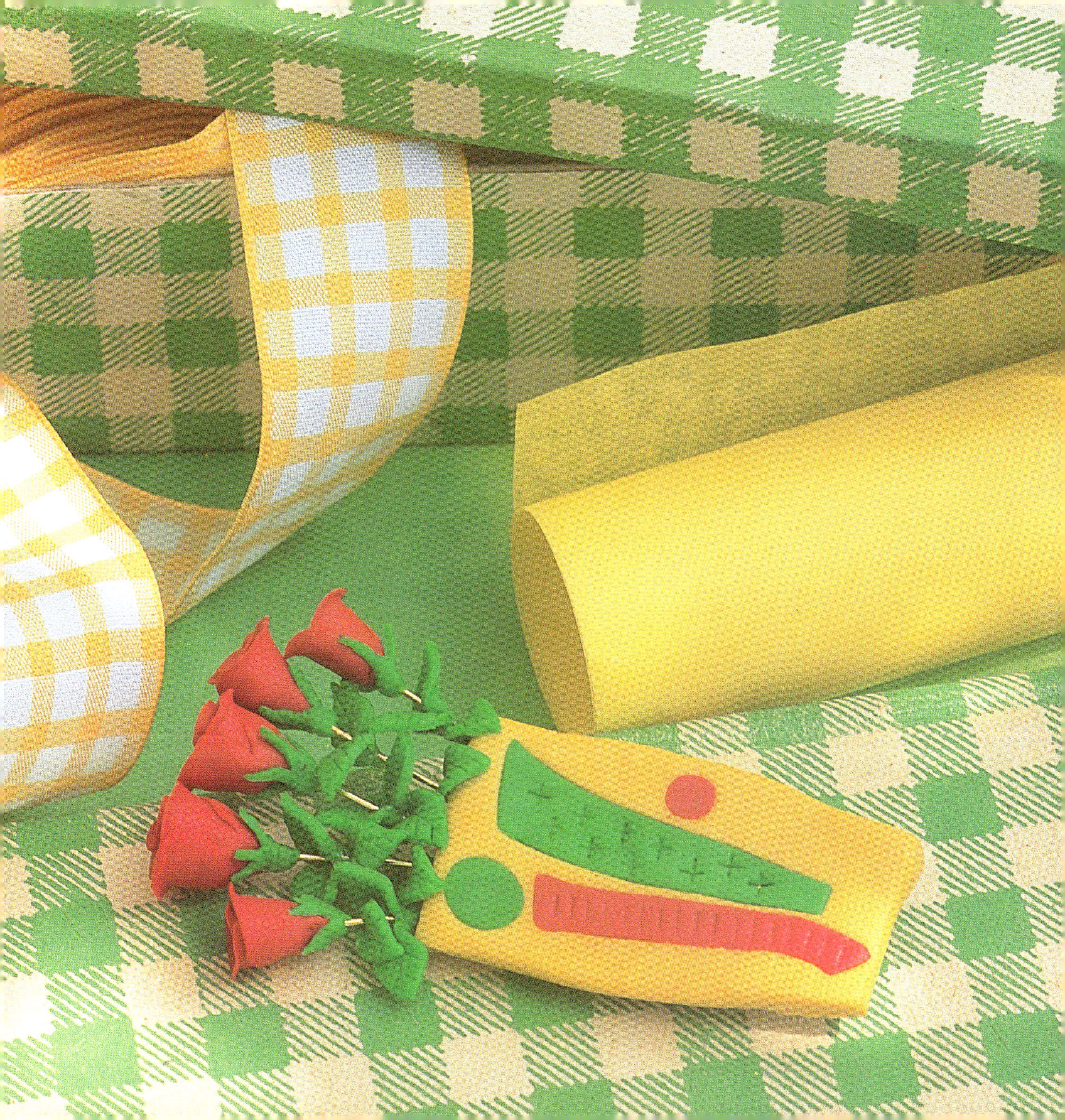

A R T   N O U V E A U   R O S E   B O X

Inspired by the early-20th-century work of the Glasgow School of Art, this design for a simple wooden box combines swirling *art nouveau* shapes and stained-glass-style roses to dramatic effect.

You Will Need

Materials
oval wooden craft box, with lid
white primer paint
acrylic paints: rose-pink, blue,
  green, yellow, white and black
clear acrylic or crackle varnish

Equipment
fine-grade sandpaper
thick bristle and fine hair
  paintbrushes
tracing paper
soft pencil
paint-mixing container

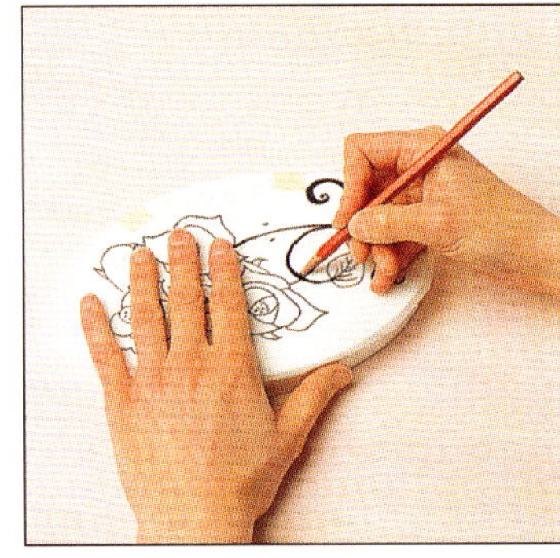

1 Sand the box and lid and give them three layers of primer. Enlarge the template from the back of the book to fit the lid of the box. Transfer it to the lid, with a soft pencil and tracing paper.

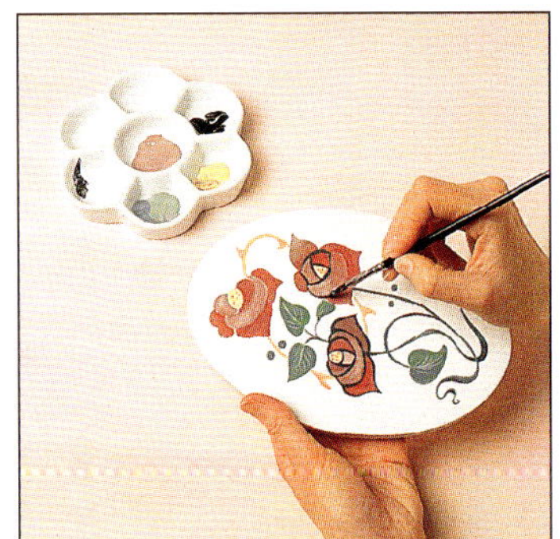

3 Paint the stems and thorn ring; add shade and tone to the flowers. Paint the veins on the leaves. Paint a black outline around the rose petals.

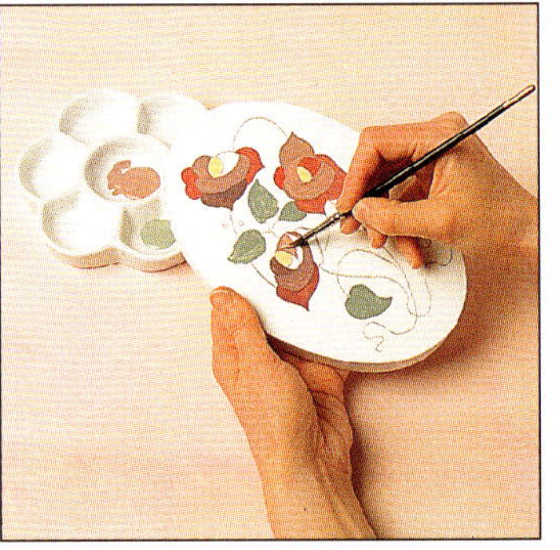

2 Paint the rose petals and the leaves as solid blocks of color.

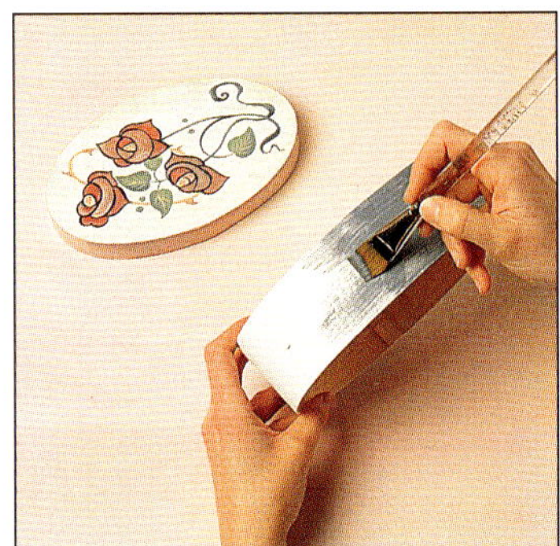

4 Color-wash the outside rim of the lid with watered-down rose paint. Paint the box blue in the same way. Seal the surface with a coat of varnish (crackle varnish will give an antique effect).

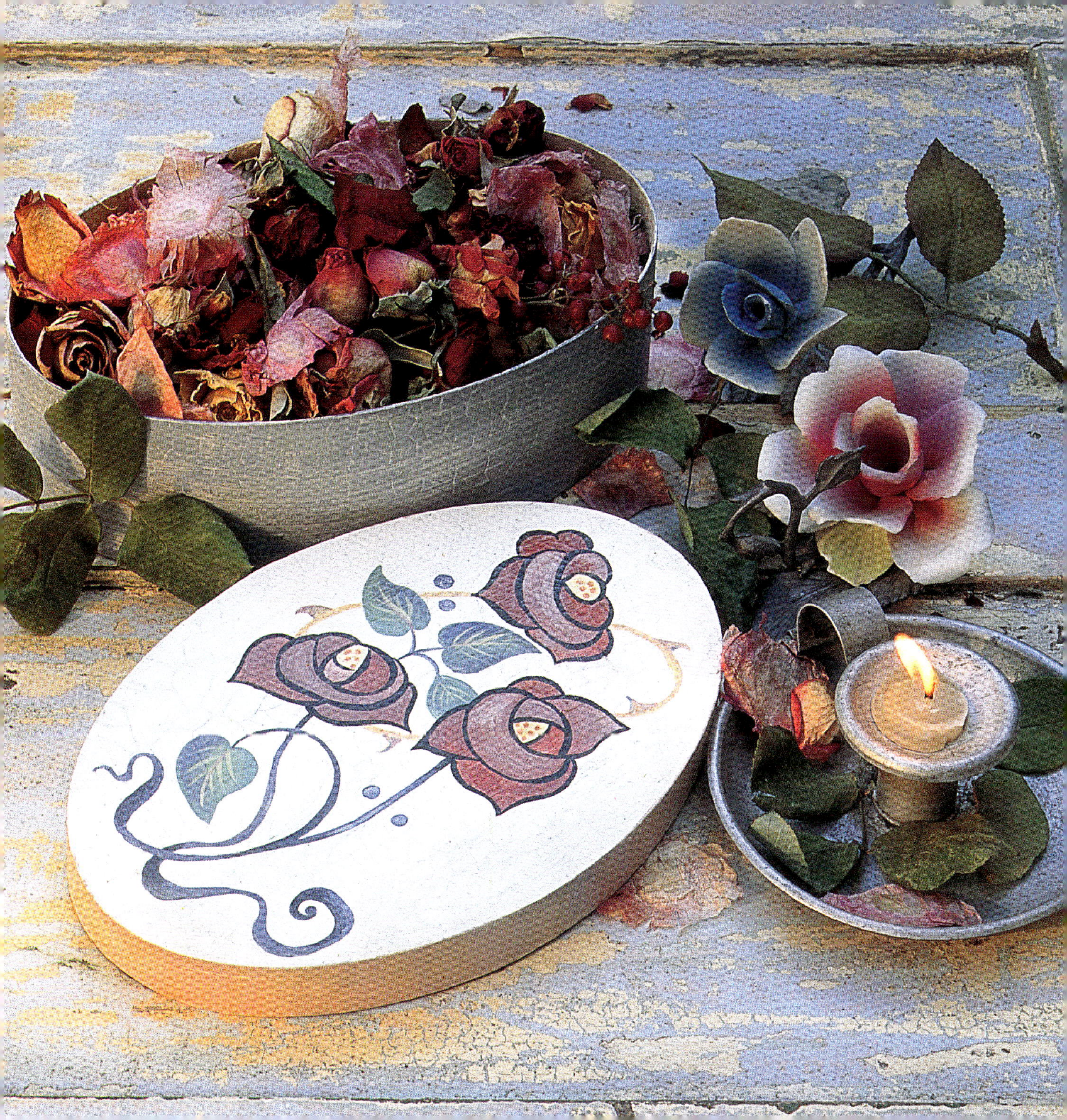

ROSE-PETAL CONFETTI BOX

This sweet little paper box makes a much prettier holder for confetti than a store-bought one, and can be kept after the wedding as a reminder of the special day.

YOU WILL NEED

MATERIALS
stiff paper or cardboard
pink paint
gold ink
double-sided tape
ribbon
rose-petal confetti

EQUIPMENT
tracing paper
pencil
scissors
paintbrush
ruler
blunt knife
cutting mat
craft knife

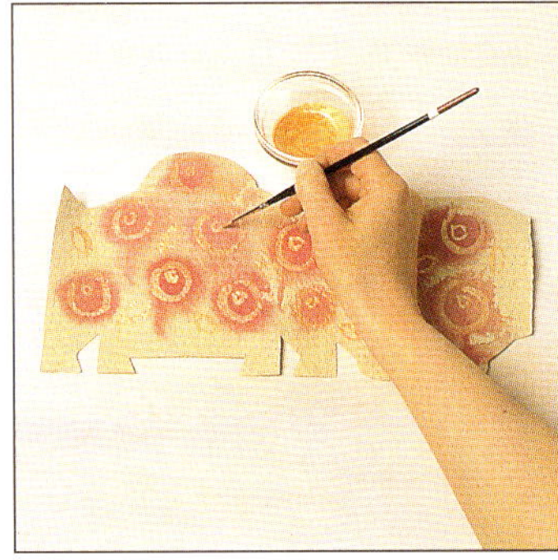

1 Trace the template for the box from the back of the book and enlarge. Lay the template on the cardboard, draw around it and cut it out. Wet the cardboard and paint rough, round pink shapes, so that the color bleeds out. Let dry. With gold ink, paint circles and leaf shapes. Let dry.

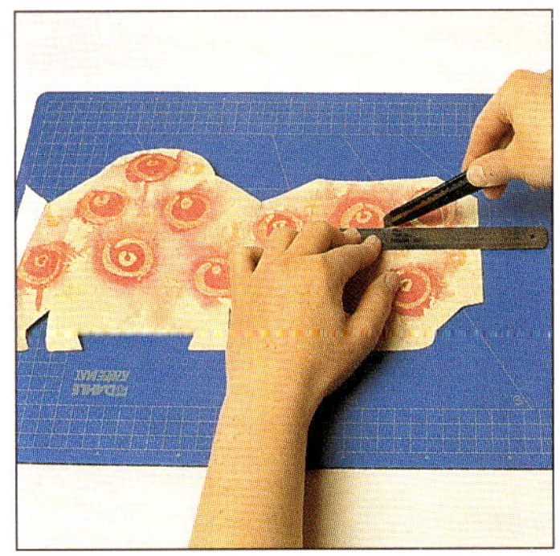

3 With a craft knife, score the slits for the ribbon.

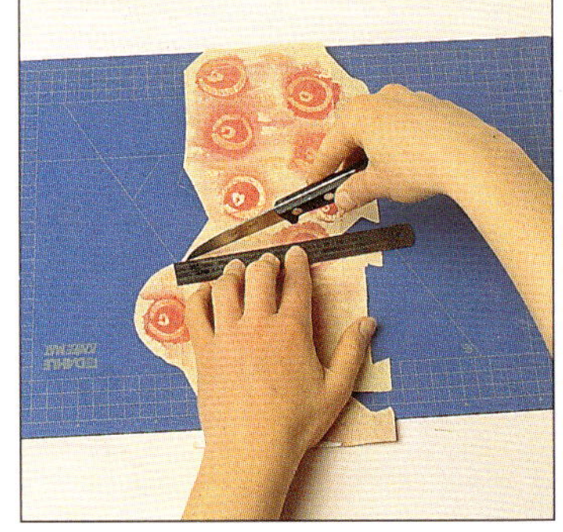

2 With a ruler and blunt knife, score the fold lines.

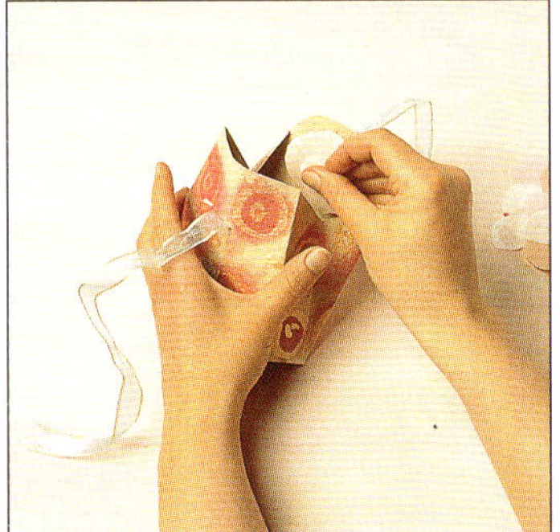

4 Cut a piece of double-sided tape and stick it to one side of the tab. Peel off the backing, overlap the tab and stick in place. Fold under the bottom edge and thread the ribbon through the slits. Fill with rose confetti and then tie the ribbon in a bow.

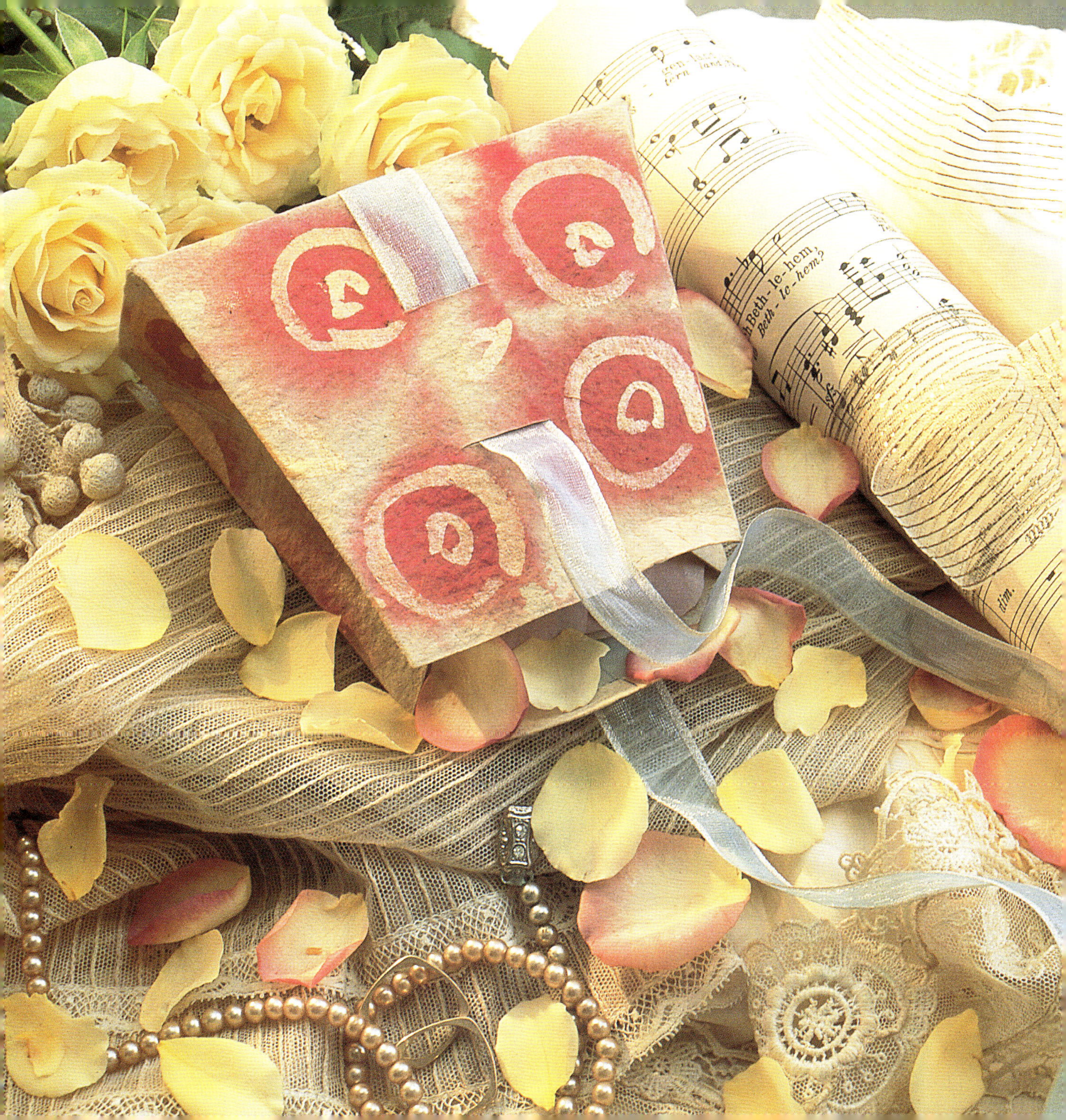

T U D O R   R O S E   C U S H I O N

The classic Tudor rose motif is picked out in quilting lines on this vibrant silk cushion; the traditional rosy red color is a perfect complement for the motif.

YOU WILL NEED

MATERIALS
red silk taffeta, 40 x 36 inches
calico, 40 x 36 inches
batting, 20 inches square
basting thread
red sewing thread
piping cord, 1½ yards
polyester stuffing

EQUIPMENT
fine black felt-tipped pen
tape measure
dressmaking scissors
quilter's pencil
needle
dressmaker's pins

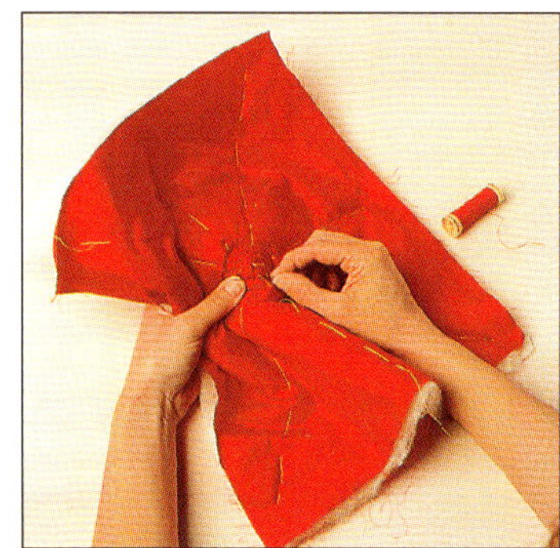

1 Trace the Tudor rose template from the back of the book, enlarging it as necessary. Outline the rose in black pen. Cut a 20-inch square of silk. Lay the silk on top and trace the rose directly onto the fabric with the quilter's pencil. Cut a 20-inch square of calico. Layer the batting between the calico and the silk. Baste the layers together with lines of stitches radiating from the center. Using red thread, quilt along the lines of the outline of the design, working from the center out. Once complete, trim the cushion along the outside lines.

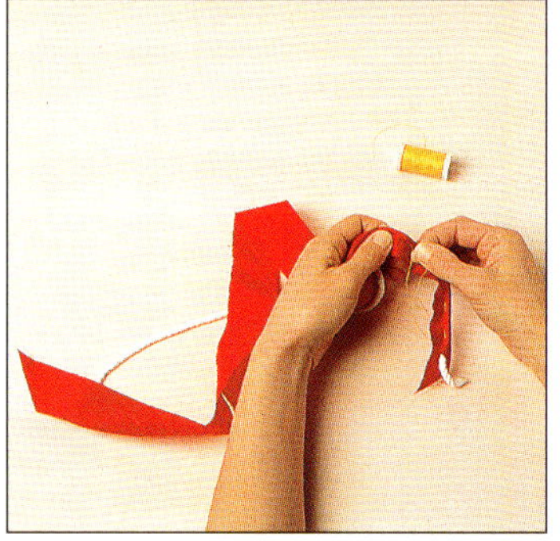

2 Cut and attach several 2-inch bias strips from the red silk. Press the seams open and trim them. Fold the bias strip over the piping cord and baste along it. Pin and baste the piping around the edge of the cushion, with the rough edges together. Machine-stitch along one side, close to the piping. Lay a square of silk and then one of calico on the right side of the cushion. Pin, baste and stitch around the edges, leaving a small gap. Trim the seams and corners and turn inside out. Fill with polyester stuffing and slip-stitch the gap closed.

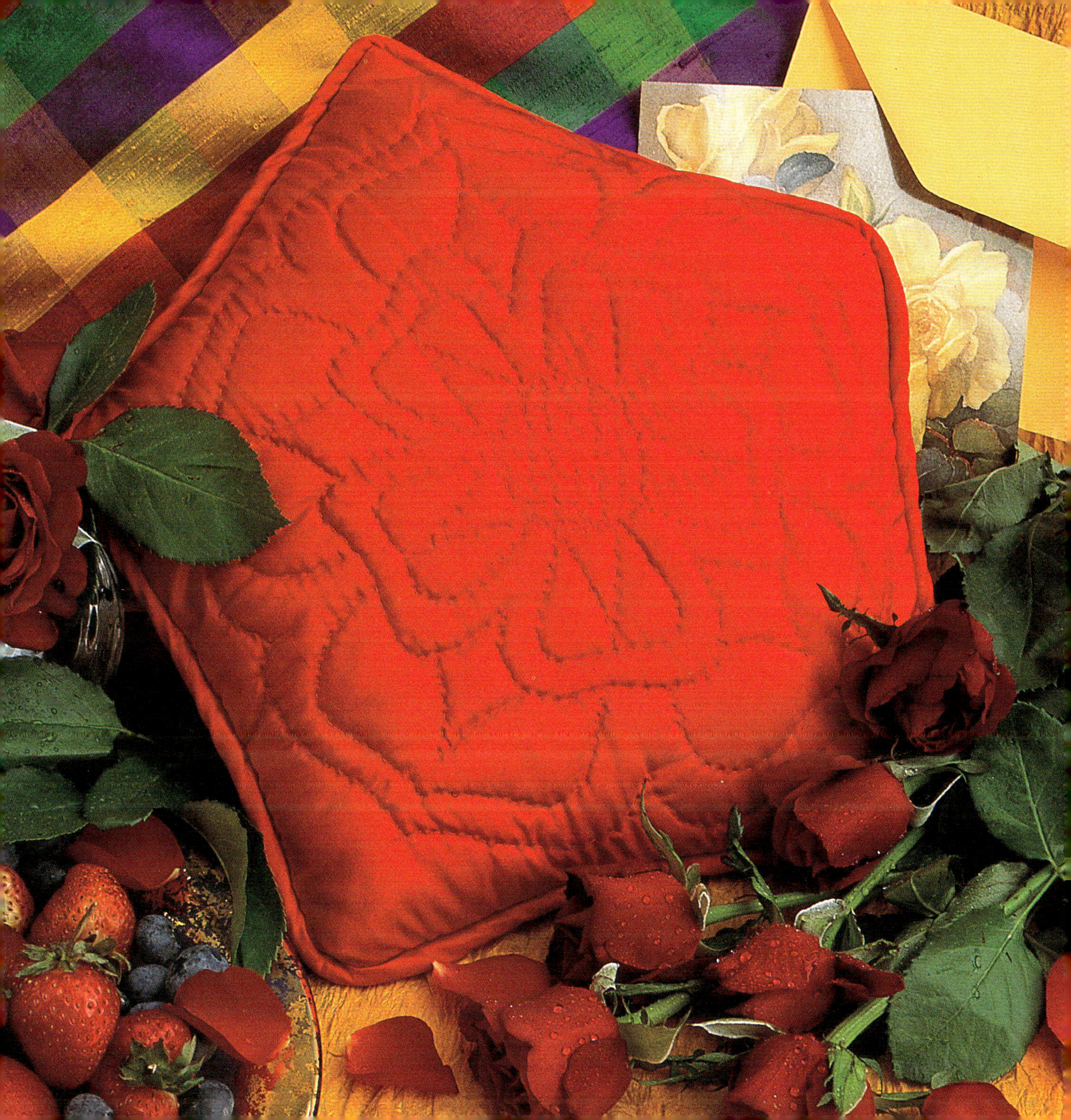

SEQUINNED ROSE BOTTLE

This ingenious technique could be used to decorate any kind of container but it is particularly suited to a tall, narrow bottle, which might otherwise be hard to work on. It would be a lovely way of presenting a bottle of rose-water as a gift.

YOU WILL NEED

MATERIALS
glass bottle
tights
matching thread
invisible thread
sequins
bugle beads
glass beads

EQUIPMENT
needle
scissors
beading needle
vanishing fabric marker

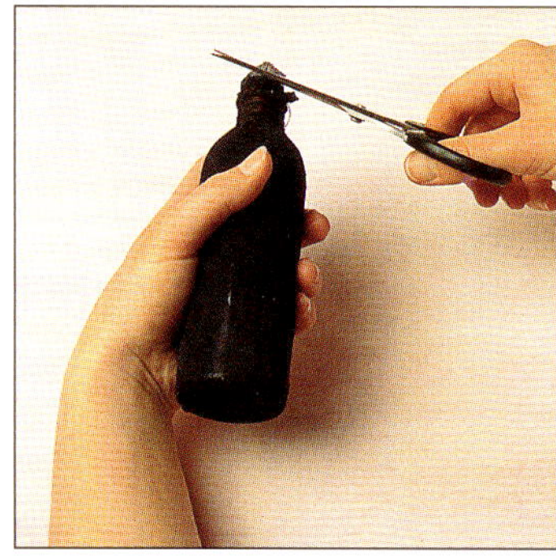

1 Place the bottle in the toe of one leg of the tights. Thread a needle with matching thread, wrap it around the neck of the bottle, secure it and trim away the excess fabric.

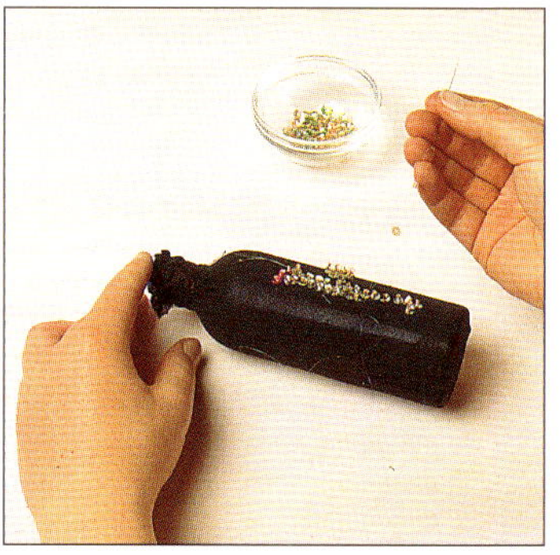

2 Thread the beading needle with invisible thread and work the rose motif: first, thread a sequin and then a bugle bead, bring the needle down and then up next to the first stitch. Continue in this fashion.

3 Draw the stripes with the marker and fill them in with sequins and glass beads, in the same way.

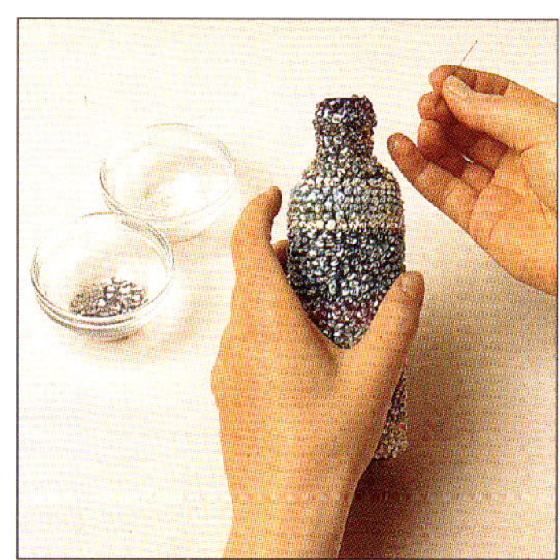

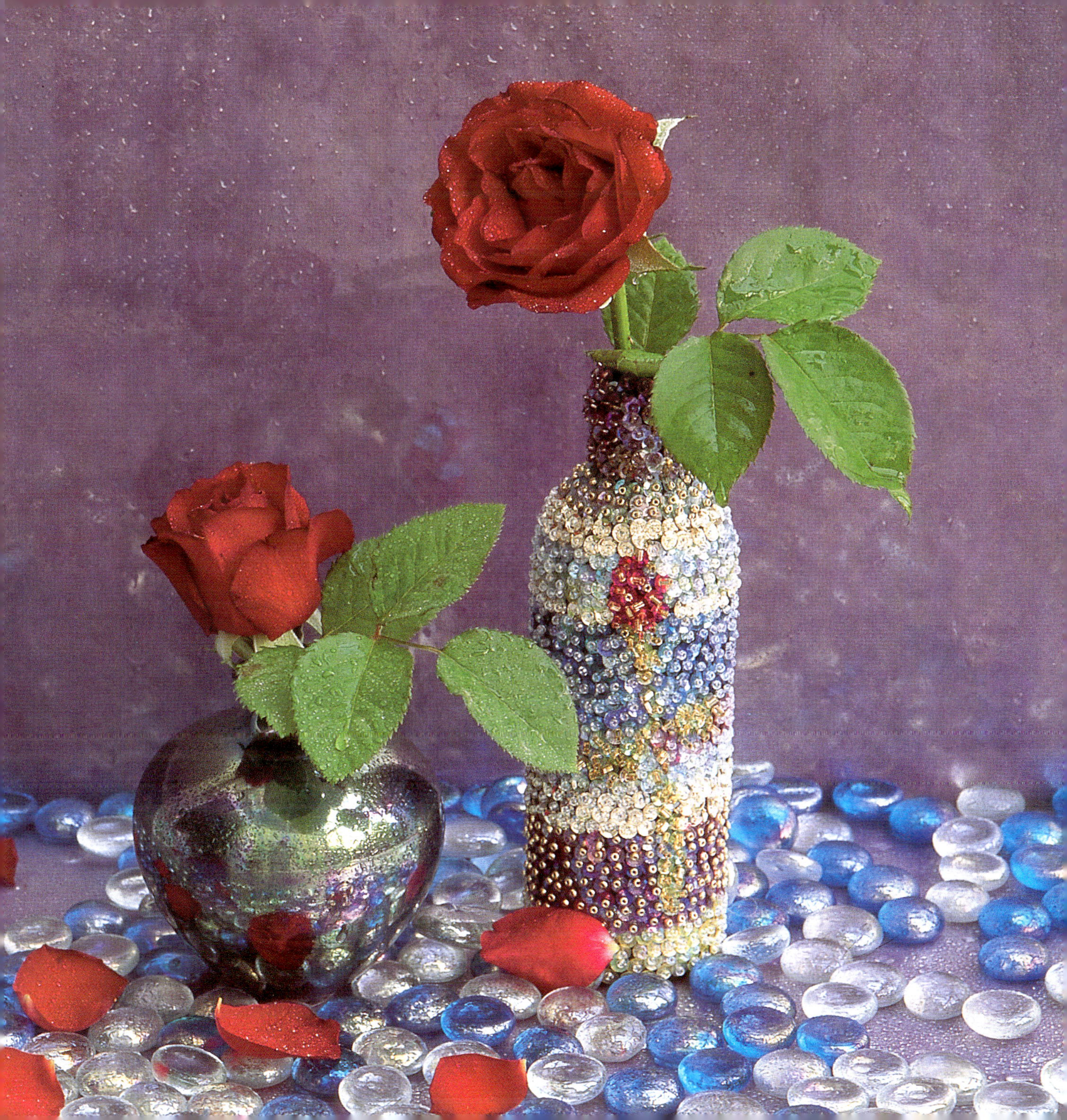

S P R A Y   O F   I C I N G   R O S E S

Incredibly realistic, this delicate spray of roses and rosebuds is easily made from the sugar paste sold for cake decorating, using a selection of clever tools. It makes a very definite statement as a cake decoration and would also be a lovely gift, presented in a beautiful box.

YOU WILL NEED

MATERIALS
*3½ ounces cyclamen flower
  paste*
*26-gauge covered
  florist's wire*
*3½ ounces green flower
  paste*
green florist's tape
ribbon, 1 yard

EQUIPMENT
rolling pin
five-petal cutter
modeling tool
foam pad
fine paintbrush
calyx cutter
set of rose-leaf cutters
toothpick
scissors

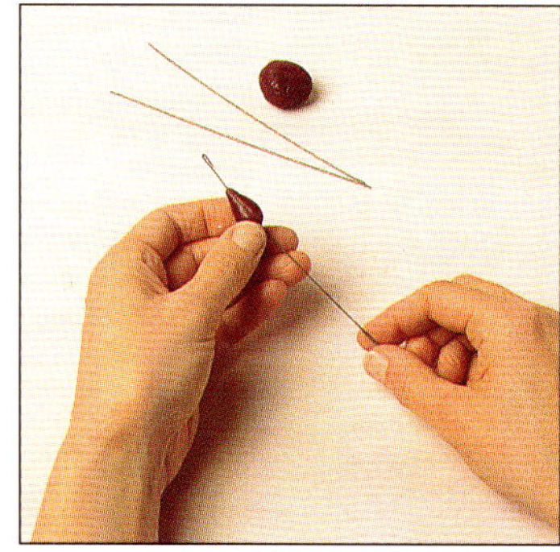

1 Roll a hazelnut-sized ball of cyclamen flower paste and mold it into a cone shape. Bend a small hook on the end of a 26-gauge wire and thread it through the top of the cone, until the loop is inside. Let dry completely.

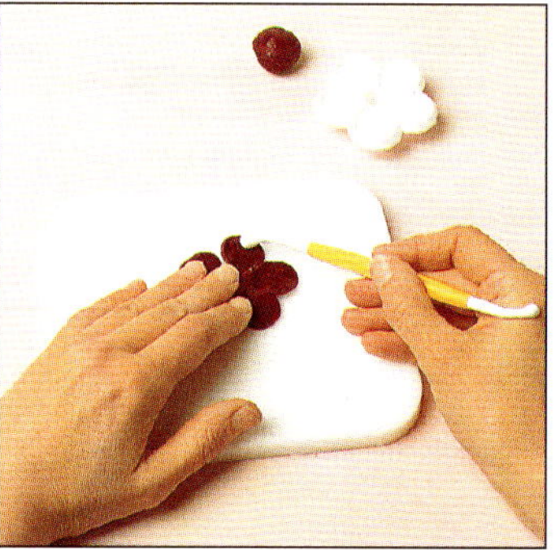

2 Roll a small piece of cyclamen flower paste fairly thinly. Cut rose petals out with the cutter and thin the edges using a dog-bone tool, resting the petal on a foam pad or in the palm of your hand.

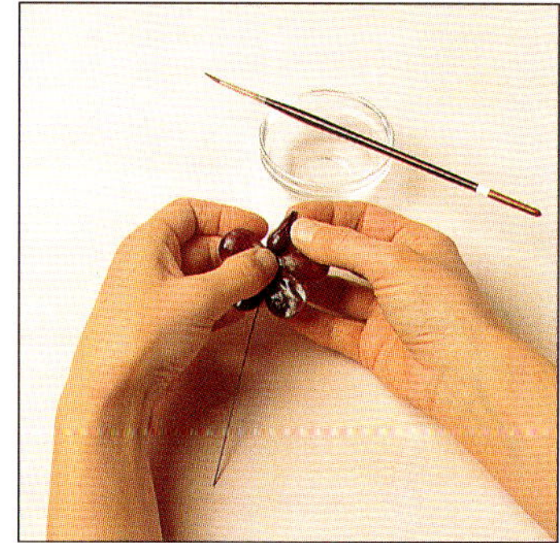

3 Insert the dry cone stem in the center of the petals. Dampen the base of each petal with a little water on a fine brush. Lift alternate petals to cling to the cone one at a time. This forms a tight rosebud, which can be opened out very carefully with a finger. Let dry. Then add additional layers of petals, if desired, to form a fuller rose.

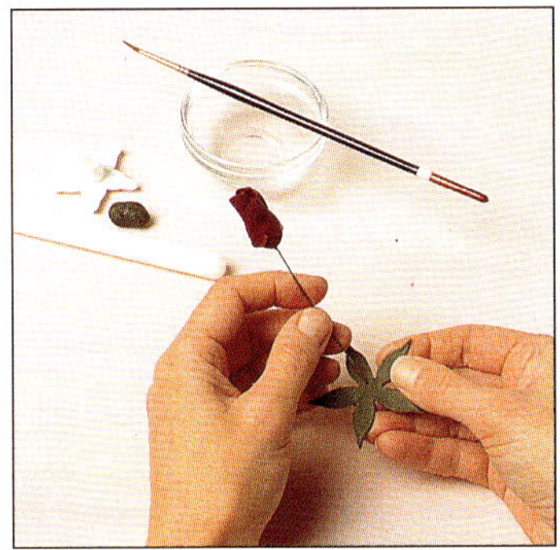

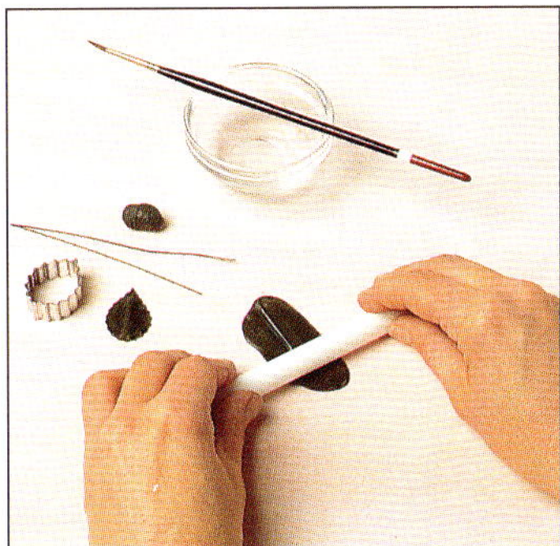

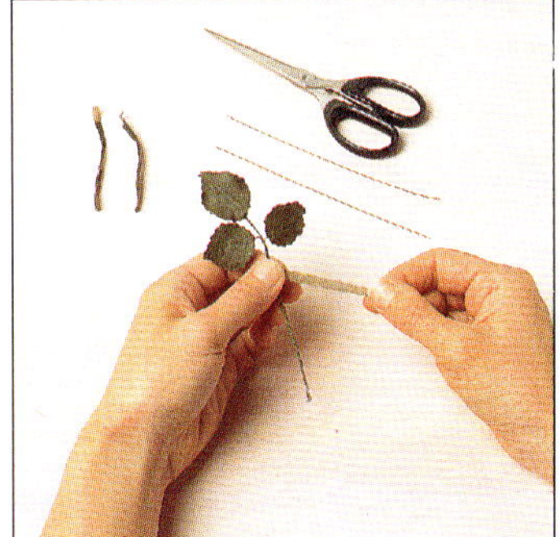

4 Roll out some green flower paste thinly. Cut a calyx with the cutter and thin the edges as before. Thread the wired rose through the center and attach it with a little water. Roll a small cone of green flower paste and thread it onto the wire, to complete the rose and calyx. Make two buds and three larger roses altogether.

5 To make the leaves, roll out some green flower paste, leaving a ridge down the middle. Cut the leaf out with a leaf cutter and mark veins with a toothpick. Holding the leaf between your finger and thumb, insert a 26 gauge wire into the ridge. Twist the leaf, to make it more realistic, and let dry.

6 Make four large leaves, 11 medium leaves and ten small leaves. Make graduated sprays of three or five leaves and tape them together, using thin strips of florist's tape.

7 Wrap a length of ribbon around to make two loops of different sizes. Trim the ends and tape on to 26-gauge wire. Cut the larger loop into two uneven lengths. Make several more ribbon loops in the same way. Arrange a leaf spray, ribbon loop and rose together and tape the stems.

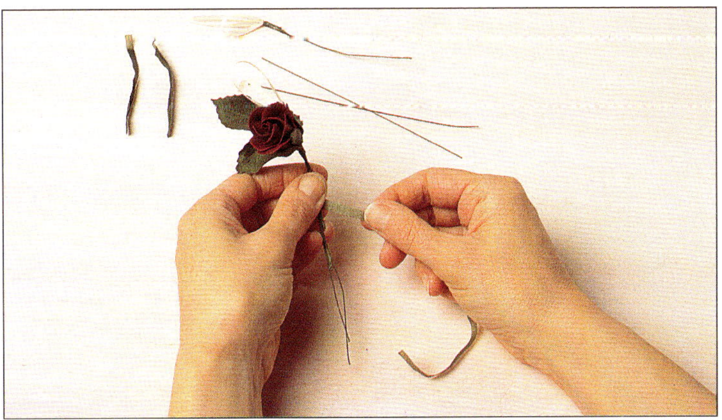

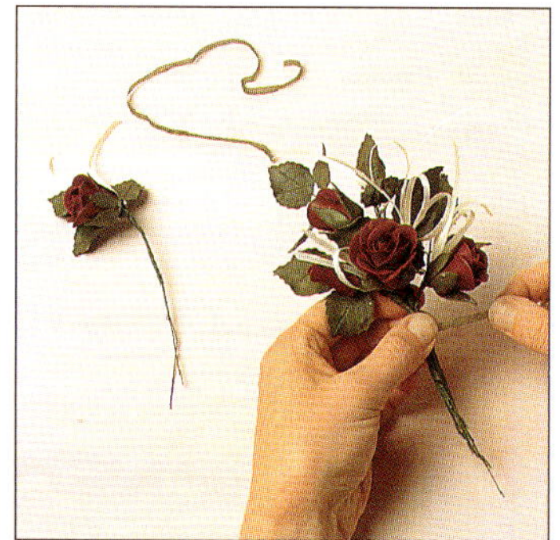

8 Beginning with a bud spray, arrange the sprays into a larger bouquet, taping the stems together as you go. Carefully bend the wires to arrange the leaves and roses attractively. Fold over the ends of the wires and wrap with tape to finish.

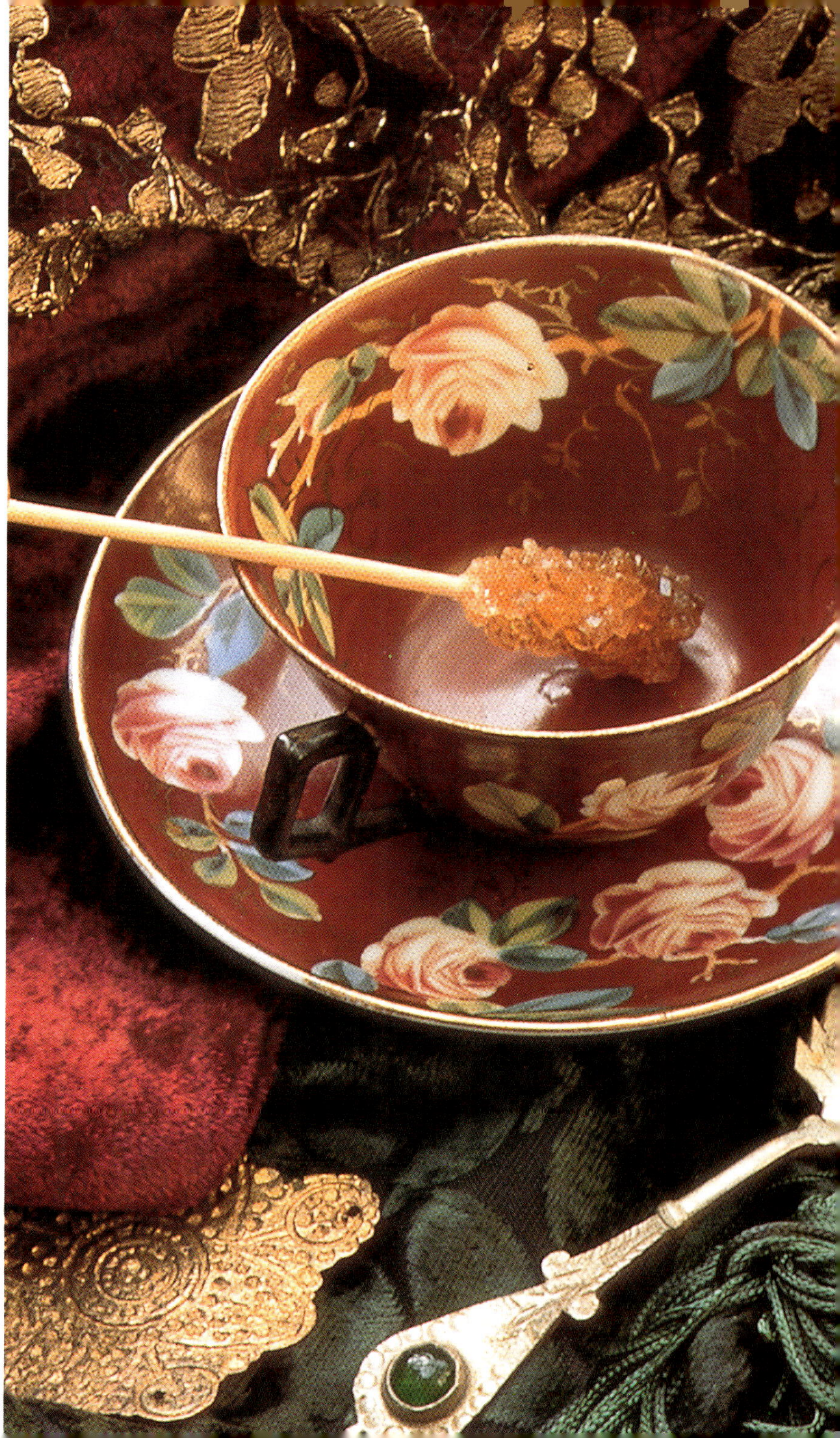

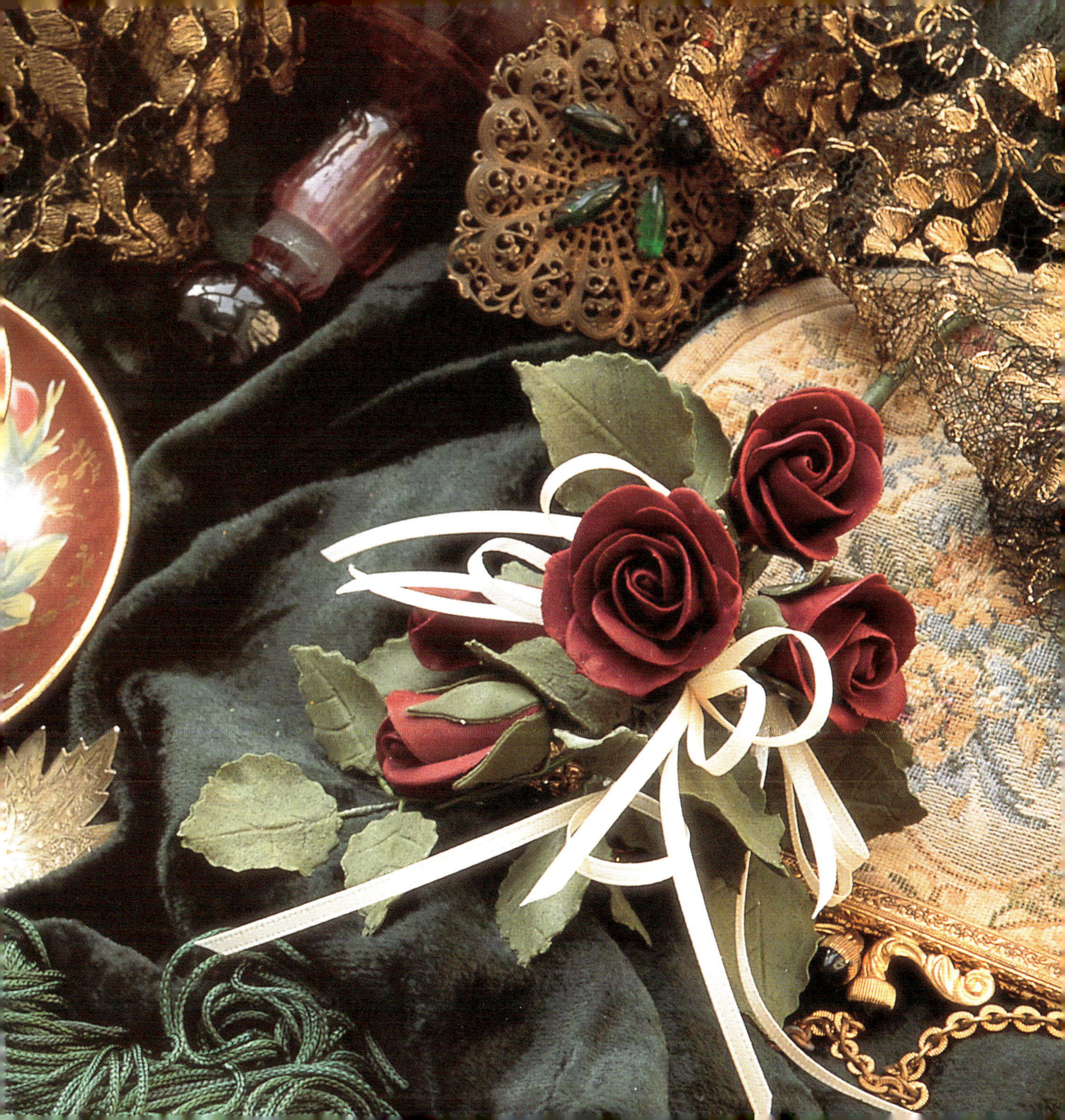

ROSE-STAMPED STATIONERY

Hand-printed stationery sends its own message, even before you have added your greetings or invitation. This golden rose would be particularly suitable for wedding stationery, making a welcome change from the usual mass-produced cards.

YOU WILL NEED

MATERIALS
linoleum square
gold paint
*blank stationery, e.g. deckle-
  edged notepaper and envelopes*
stationery box
Japanese paper, cut into strips
ribbon

EQUIPMENT
tracing paper
pencil
linoleum-cutting tools
small paint roller
fine paintbrush
metal ruler
glue stick

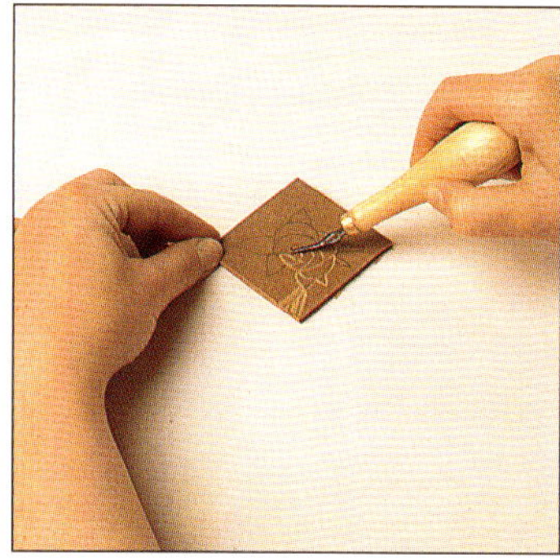

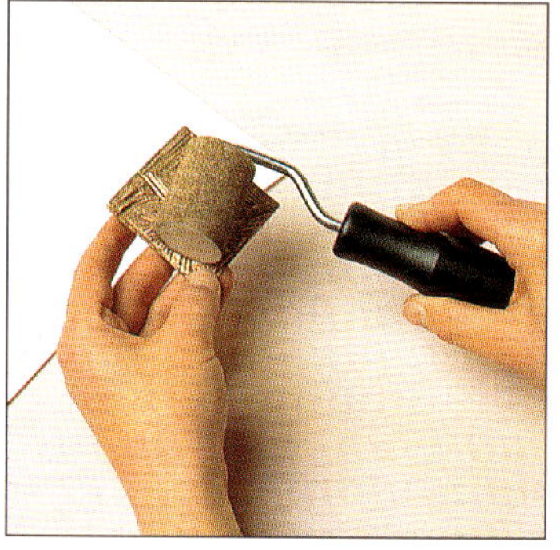

1 Trace the rose motif from the back of the book, enlarging it as desired. Transfer to the linoleum. Using a narrow-grooved tool, cut out the motif, keeping your free hand behind the blade at all times. With a wide tool, cut away the excess linoleum. Indicate with an arrow which edge is the top, on the back.

2 Ink the linoleum stamp with gold paint and stamp the stationery, re-inking the roller each time. Wipe away any build-up of paint.

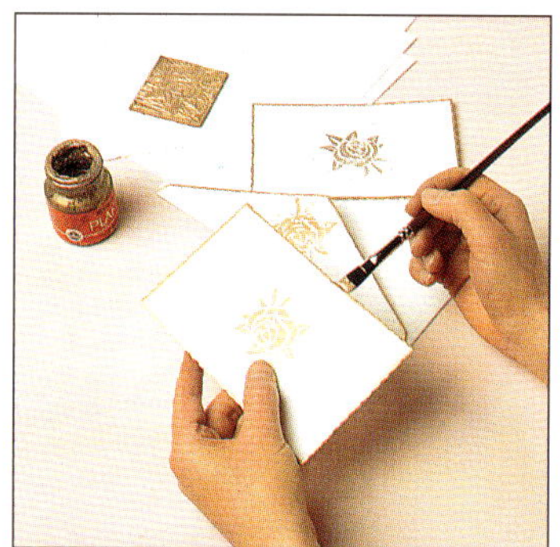

3 Edge the envelopes, cards and the top edge of the notepaper with a fine line of gold paint. Glue the box with strips of Japanese paper. Arrange the notepaper and cards in the box. Bind the envelopes with more Japanese paper and ribbon and add them to the box. Decorate the box lid with ribbon.

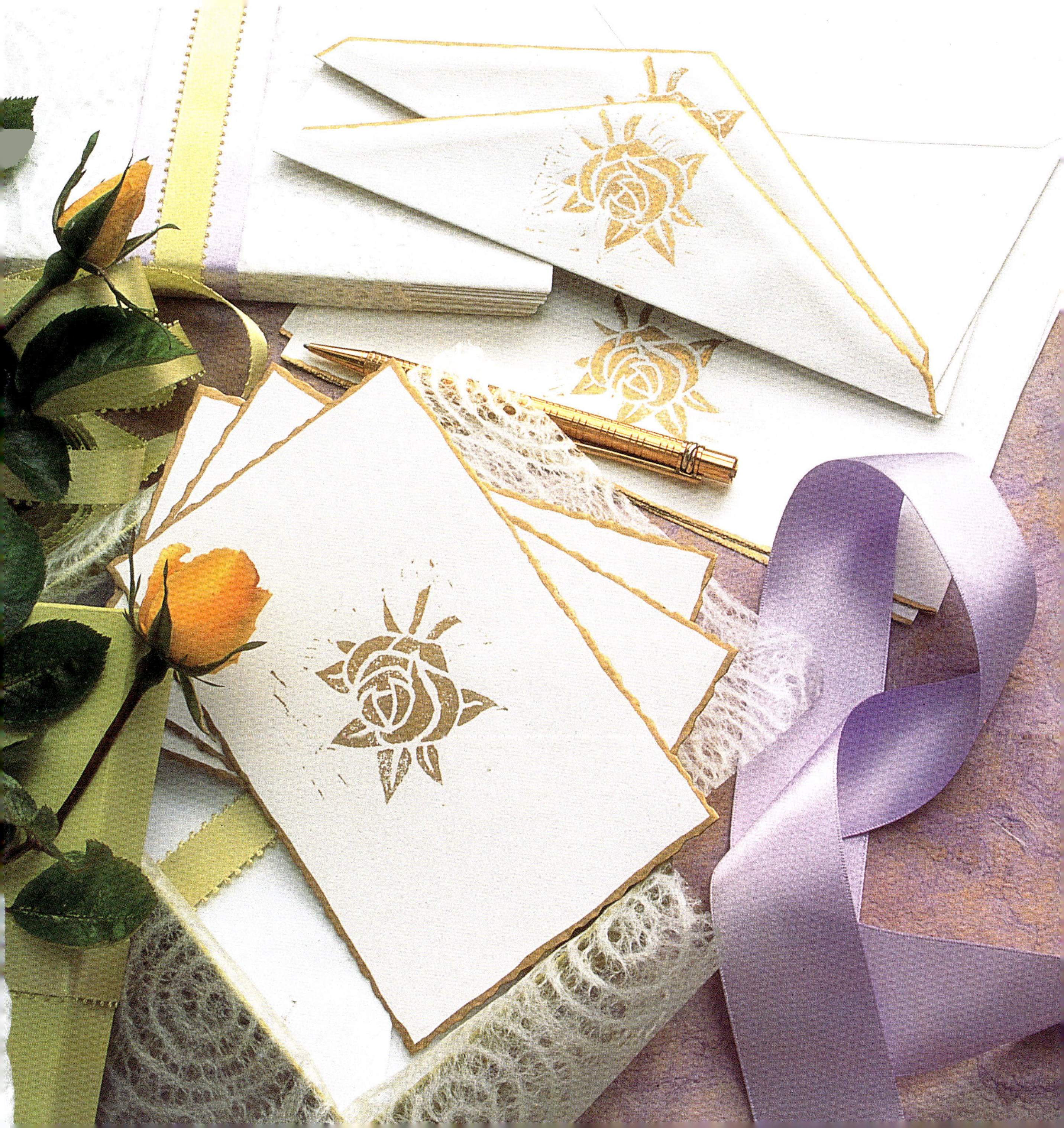

ROSE-STENCILED TABLECLOTH

Two stencils are arranged here to decorate a square tablecloth; the same motifs could be used in many different combinations and scales. Use two or three shades with each stencil shape to achieve a rounded, three-dimensional look to the roses, leaves and branches.

YOU WILL NEED

MATERIALS
heavy white cotton fabric,
* 30 inches square*
stencil paints: dark pink,
* pale pink, yellow, dark green,*
* light green and warm brown*
white sewing thread

EQUIPMENT
stencil paper
stencil cardboard
craft knife
cutting mat
iron
spray adhesive
3 stencil brushes
vanishing fabric marker
long ruler
set square
needle

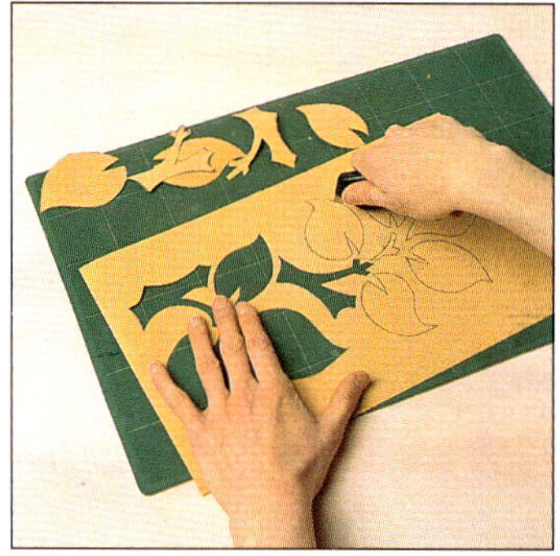

1 Enlarge the rose template from the back of the book so that it measures 6 inches across. Enlarge the branch template so that it is 12 inches long. Transfer both onto the stencil cardboard and carefully cut out the stencils, with the knife, on the cutting mat.

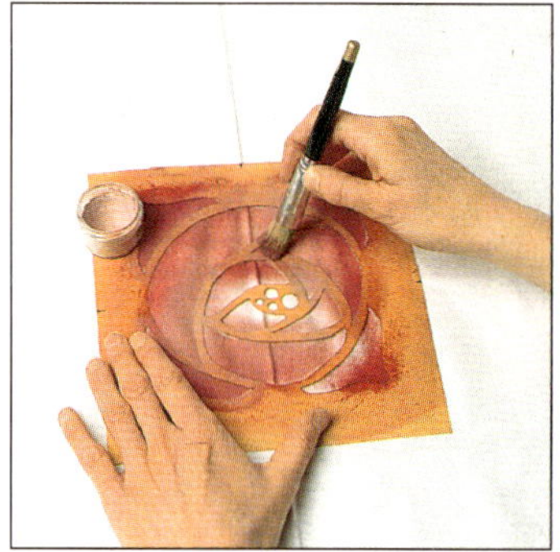

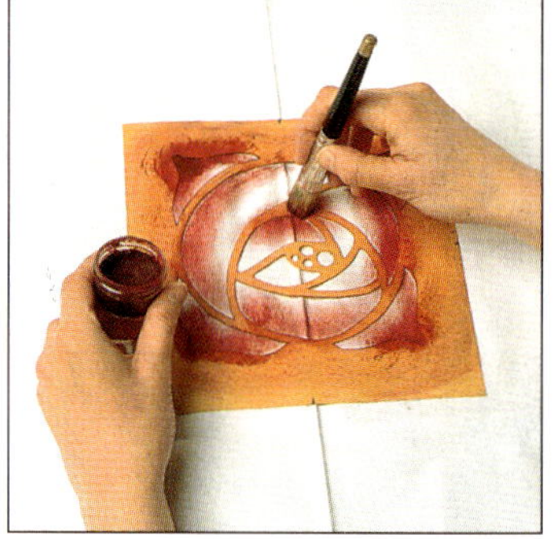

2 Fold the fabric in half each way, to find the center. Press lightly along the creases. Spray the back of the rose stencil lightly with adhesive and place it in the middle of the cloth. Start with dark pink paint in the corner petals and around the outer edge of the inner petals.

3 Fill in the rest of the petals with pale pink and color the center dots in yellow. Keep the brush upright and use a small circling motion to transfer the paint. Be careful not to overload the bristles. Peel off the stencil and let the paint dry.

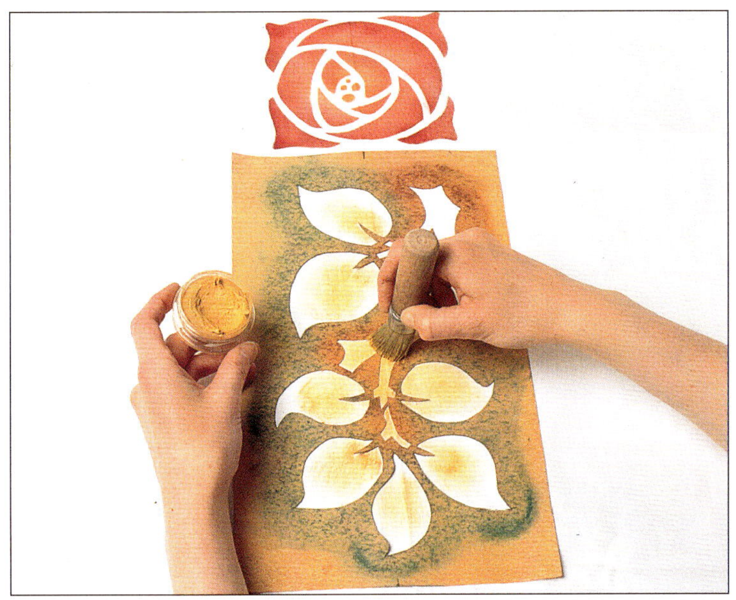

4 Work a branch motif on each side of the rose, using the crease as a placement guide, to form a cross. Spray the back of the card with adhesive, as before. Stencil yellow paint in the center of each leaf.

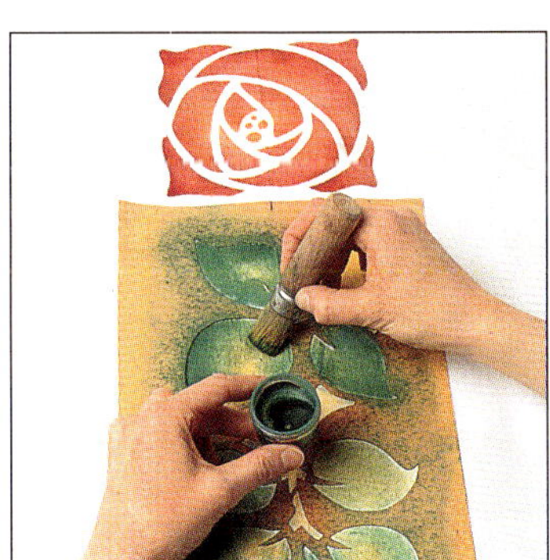

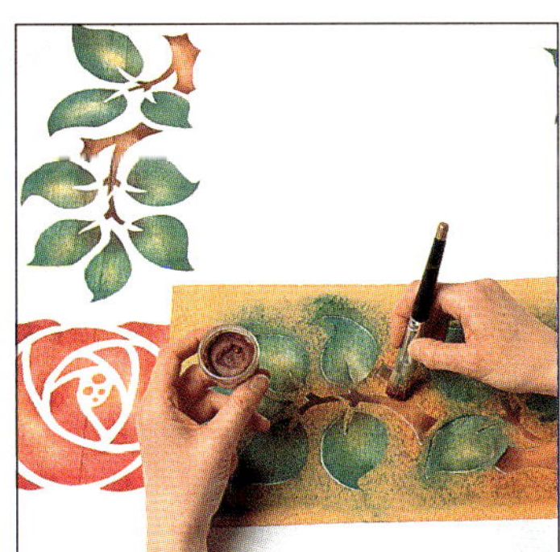

5 Blend dark and light green paints and finish painting the leaves.

6 Work a small amount of brown around the base of the leaves and the outside edge of the branches. Stencil a rose at the end of each branch. With a fabric marker, and using the ruler and set square to get a perfectly accurate square, draw a line about 6 inches from each edge, so that it is on the same level as the outer edge of the roses. Stencil a rose in each corner and then work a branch between the roses.

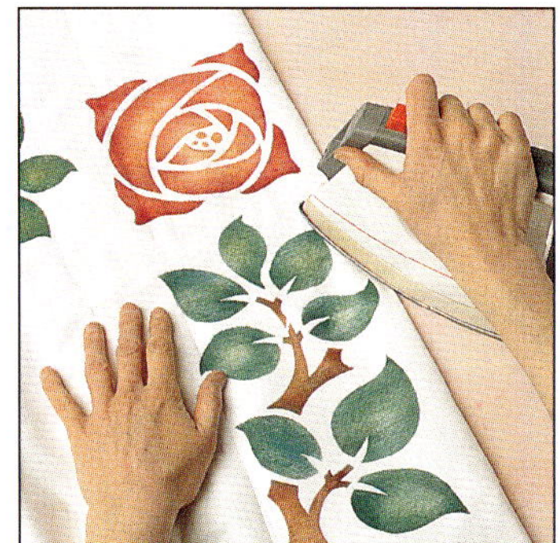

7 When the paint is quite dry, set it according to the manufacturer's instructions. Turn under, press and stitch a narrow double hem along the outside edge.

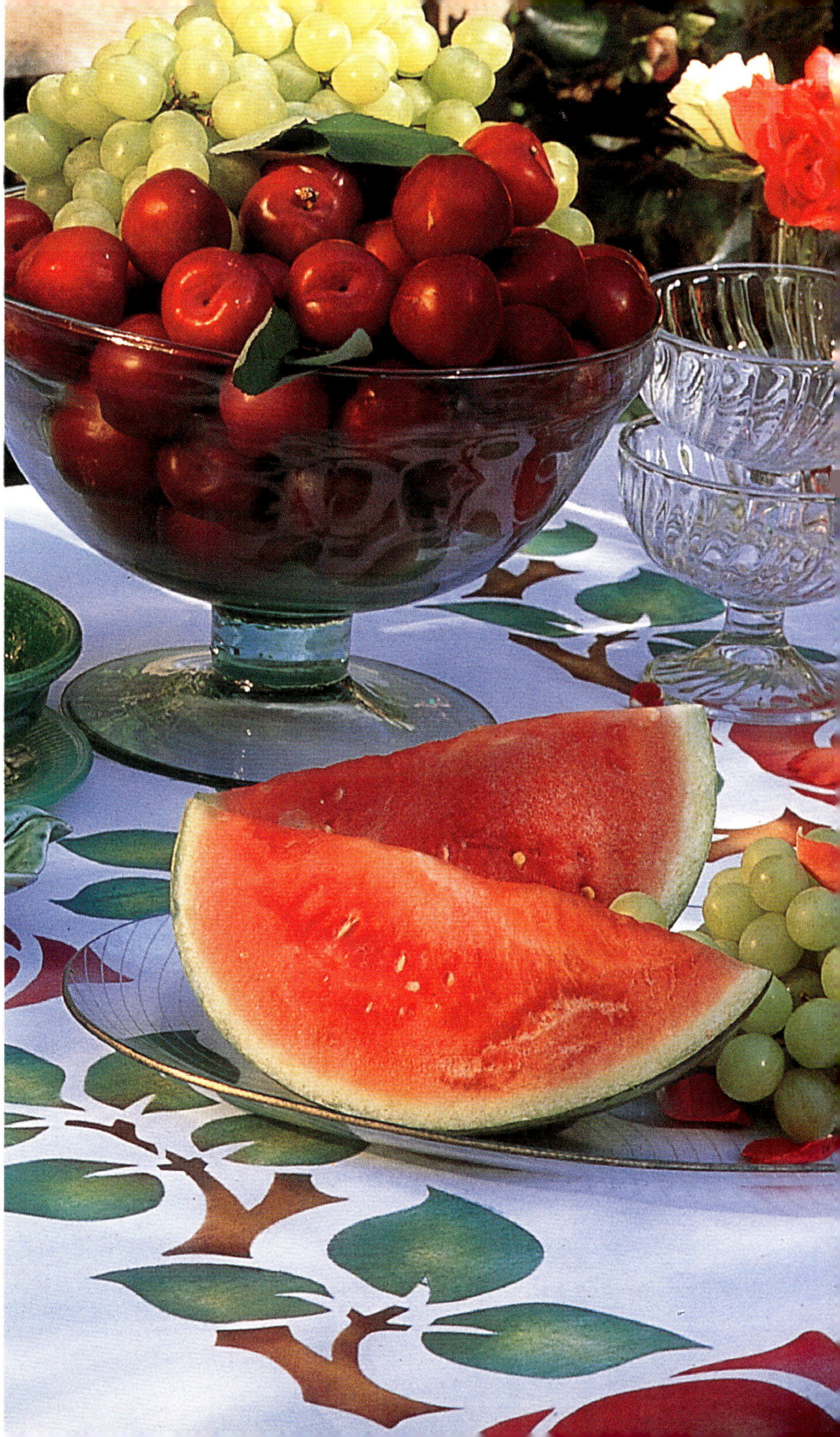

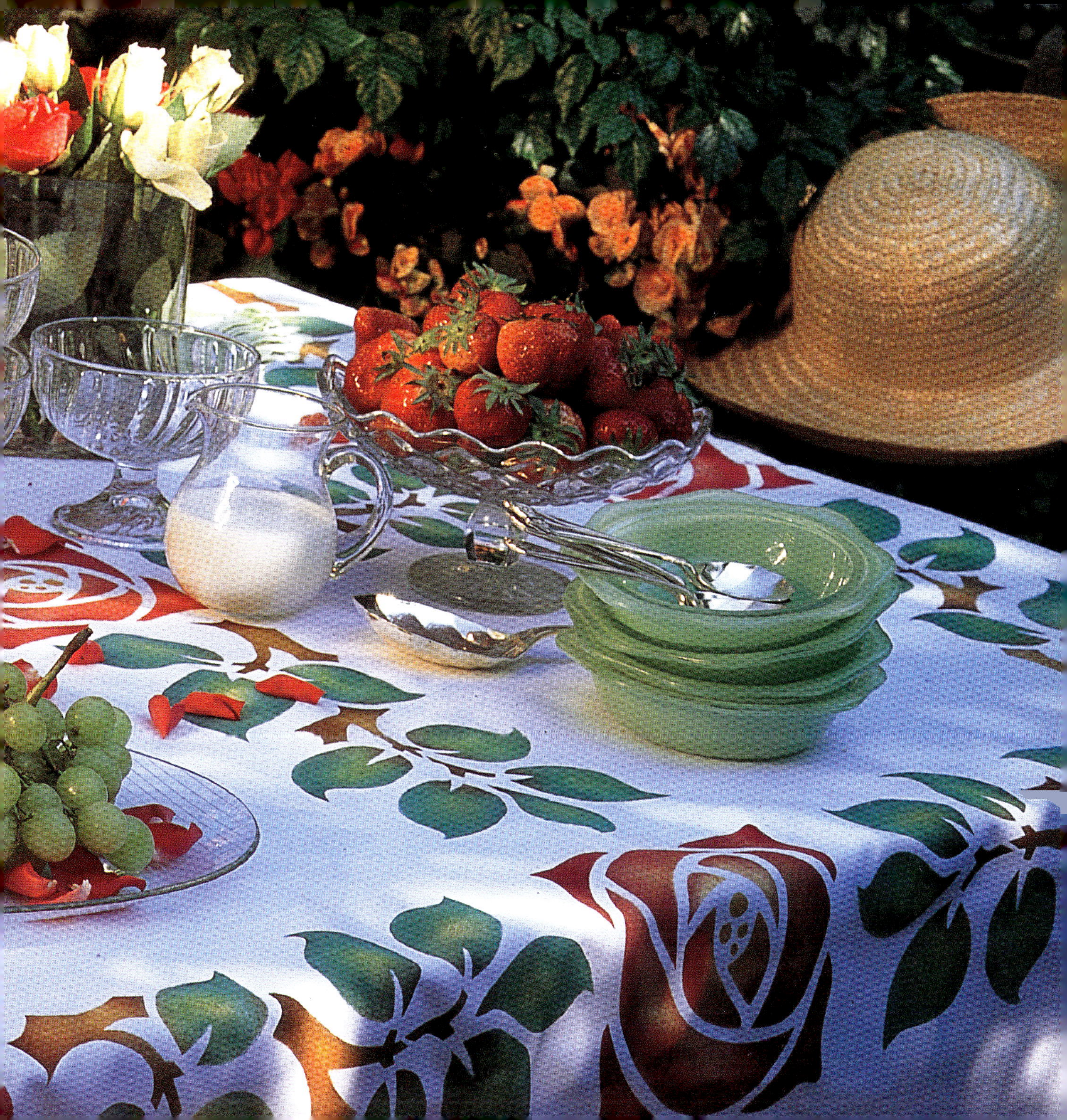

WATER-RESISTANT ROSE TABLEMAT

Here a very traditional and popular motif is depicted in bright, bold, contemporary colors.

YOU WILL NEED

MATERIALS
light gray Zweigart Annable evenweave canvas fabric, 15 x 22 inches
matching and black sewing thread
Anchor "Marlitt" shades 836, 815, 801 and 1032
basting thread

EQUIPMENT
tape measure
scissors
dressmaker's pins
sewing machine
iron
needle
tracing paper
pencil

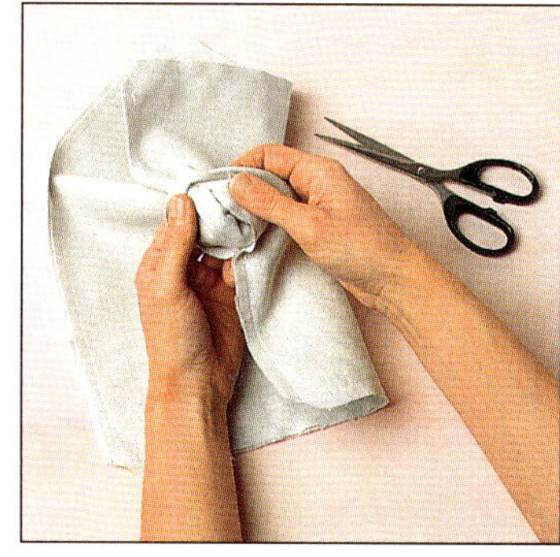

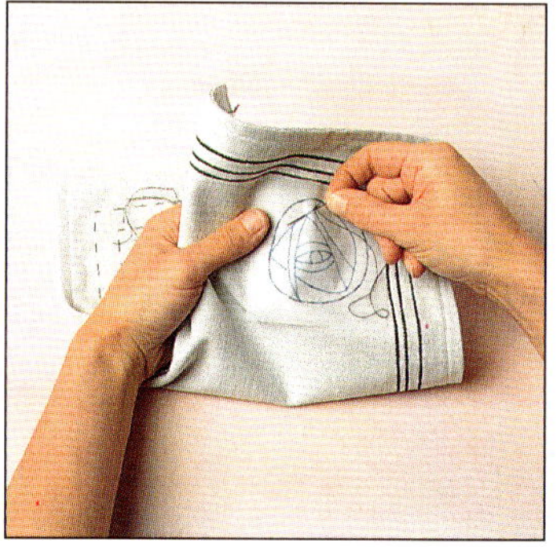

1 Cut two 11 x 15-inch rectangles from the evenweave fabric. Pin together and stitch around the edges, ⅝ inch from the edge, using the matching thread and leaving a gap on one side. Miter the corners, turn right-side out and press.

Top-stitch ½ inch from the edge. Baste guidelines around the edge of the mat, 1 inch and 1½ inches from the edge. Machine zigzag stitch over the top of the guidelines, using black thread. Use the presser foot as a guide to stitch the crosswise lines. Stitch in the thread ends on the reverse side.

2 Trace the motif from the back of the book. Pin in position. Baste around the lines, then tear the paper away. Machine zigzag along the lines and sew in the ends.

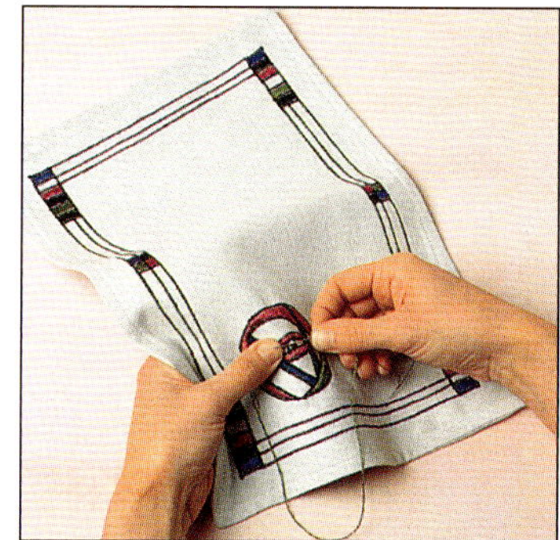

3 Fill in the colored areas of the border in satin stitch, using two strands of Persian thread. Ease the satin stitches on the rose to fit around the curves and fill in the center.

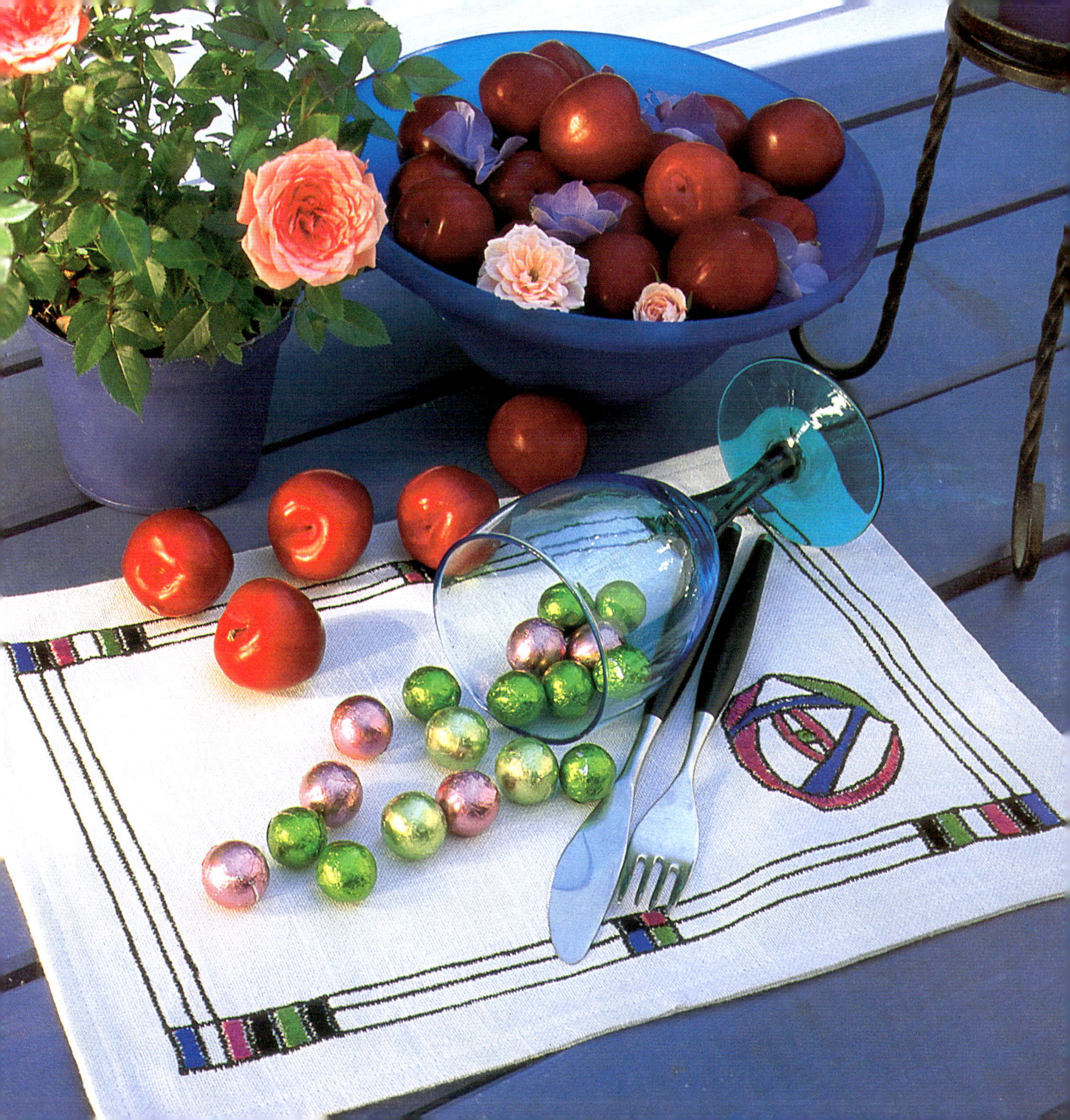

RIBBON ROSE HAIRBAND

Choose ribbons to match a bridesmaid's outfit or a special party dress. With practice, these pretty ribbon roses will be easy to make.

YOU WILL NEED

MATERIALS
satin-covered padded hairband
15-inch lengths of 1½ -inch-wide
* gauze and satin ribbons*
24-inch length of 2½-inch
* wide tartan ribbon*
2 yards of 1½-inch-wide
* sheer green plain and gold-*
* edged ribbons*
matching sewing thread

EQUIPMENT
needle
scissors

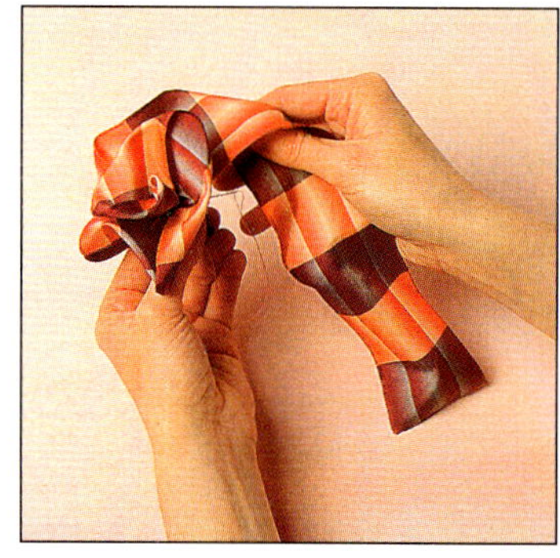

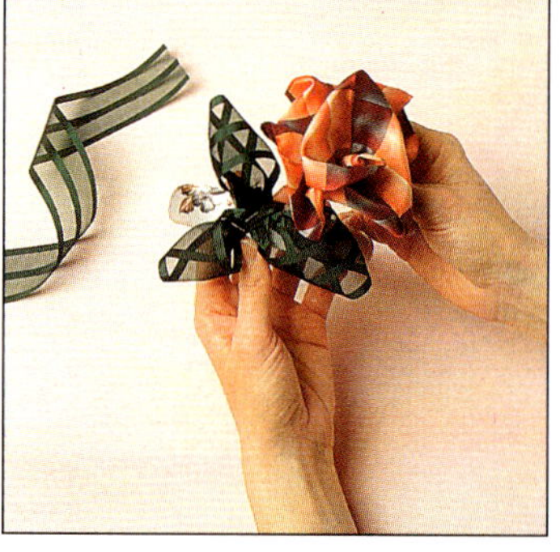

1 Make the central rose first. Fold one end of tartan ribbon at a right angle and twist it around twice, to form the center. Secure at the bottom with a few stitches. Form the first petal by twisting the ribbon around the center, folding it back at a right angle, so that the top edge lies across the "stalk", and attach it with a secure stitch. Continue to wrap the ribbon around in this way, securing each petal with a stitch. Finish off firmly, by stitching through all the layers.

2 Cut the green ribbon into 6-inch lengths and fold them to make leaves. Sew them to the center of the hairband and then attach the rose in the middle.

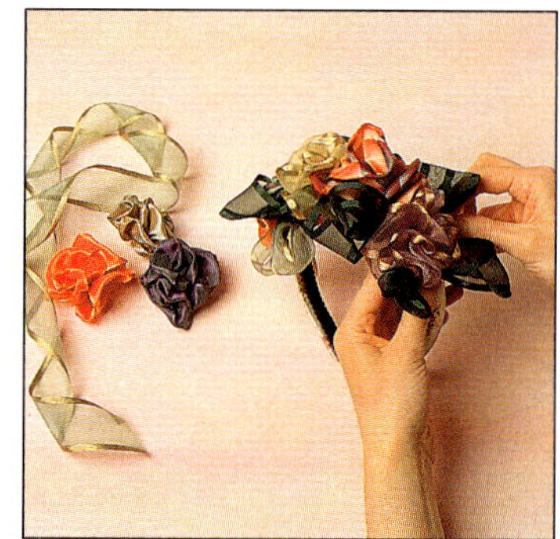

3 Make six more roses in different colors and sew them along the hairband, interspersing them with more green leaves in plain and gold-edged ribbon.

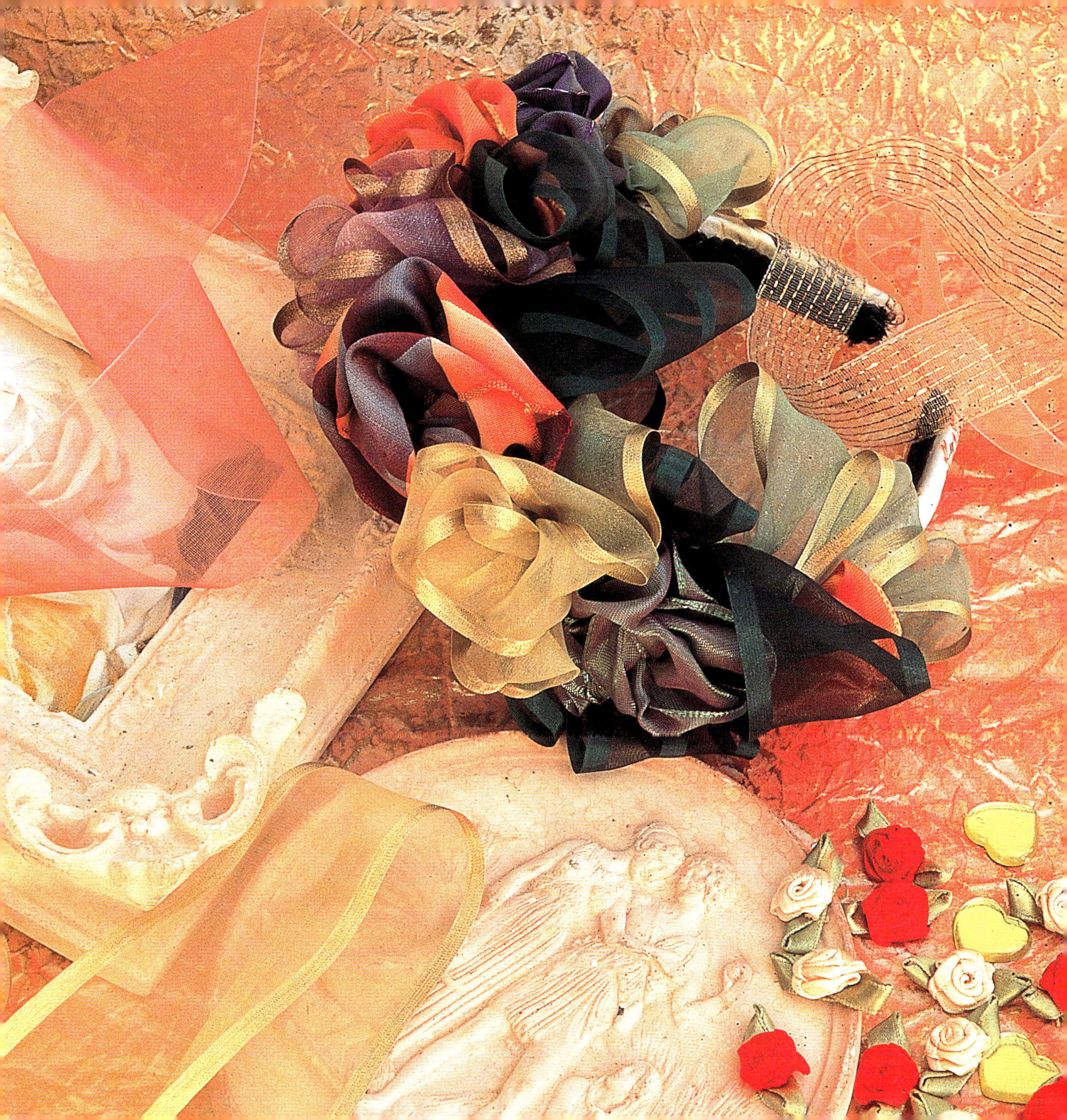

ROSE JEWELRY POUCH

The intense, dark red of the velvet provides a suitable setting for your most precious jewels, but it also evokes the softness and tonal contrasts of rose petals, which are stylized into a free-embroidered motif to decorate the pouch.

YOU WILL NEED

MATERIALS
batting
dark red velvet
taffeta lining fabric
matching sewing thread
velvet ribbon
small button

EQUIPMENT
dressmaker's pins
sewing machine, with darning foot
tracing paper
pencil
needle
paper and round template
tape measure
dressmaking scissors

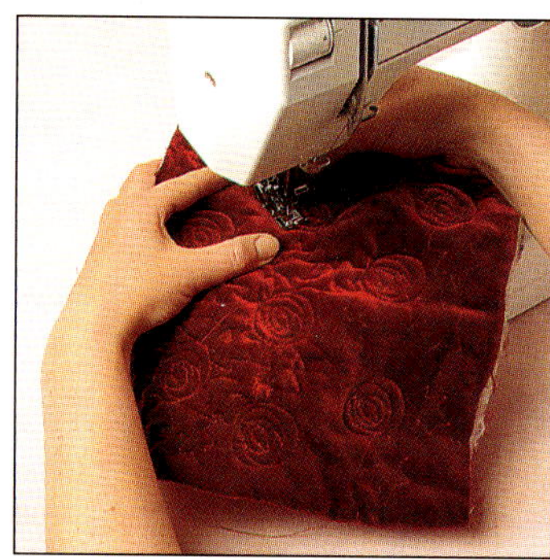

1 Cut out 15 x 10-inch pieces of batting, velvet and lining fabric. Assemble and pin together with the velvet in the middle. Stitch seams across the top and bottom. Turn right-sides out so the batting is inside and pin the top and bottom seams. Trace the template from the back of the book and enlarge it, if necessary. Transfer the rose and leaf motifs to the fabric. Select the darning or free embroidery mode on your sewing machine and attach the darning foot. Stitch the design.

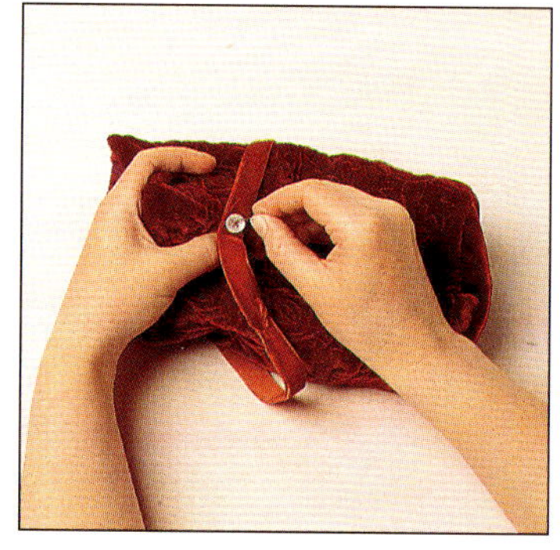

2 With right sides together, stitch the two short edges together to form a tube, leaving the lining unstitched. Fold under the lining and slip-stitch the edges together. Make a paper template for a circle with 3-inch radius. Use it to cut pieces of velvet and taffeta to this size. With right sides together, stitch around the seam allowance, leaving a 1½-inch gap. Clip the seam allowance and turn the circle the right way out. Hand-stitch the circle to the bottom edge of the tube. Cut a piece of velvet ribbon 16 inches long. Stitch the centerpoint to the side seam of the bag. Sew a small button in place.

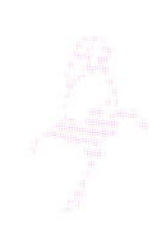

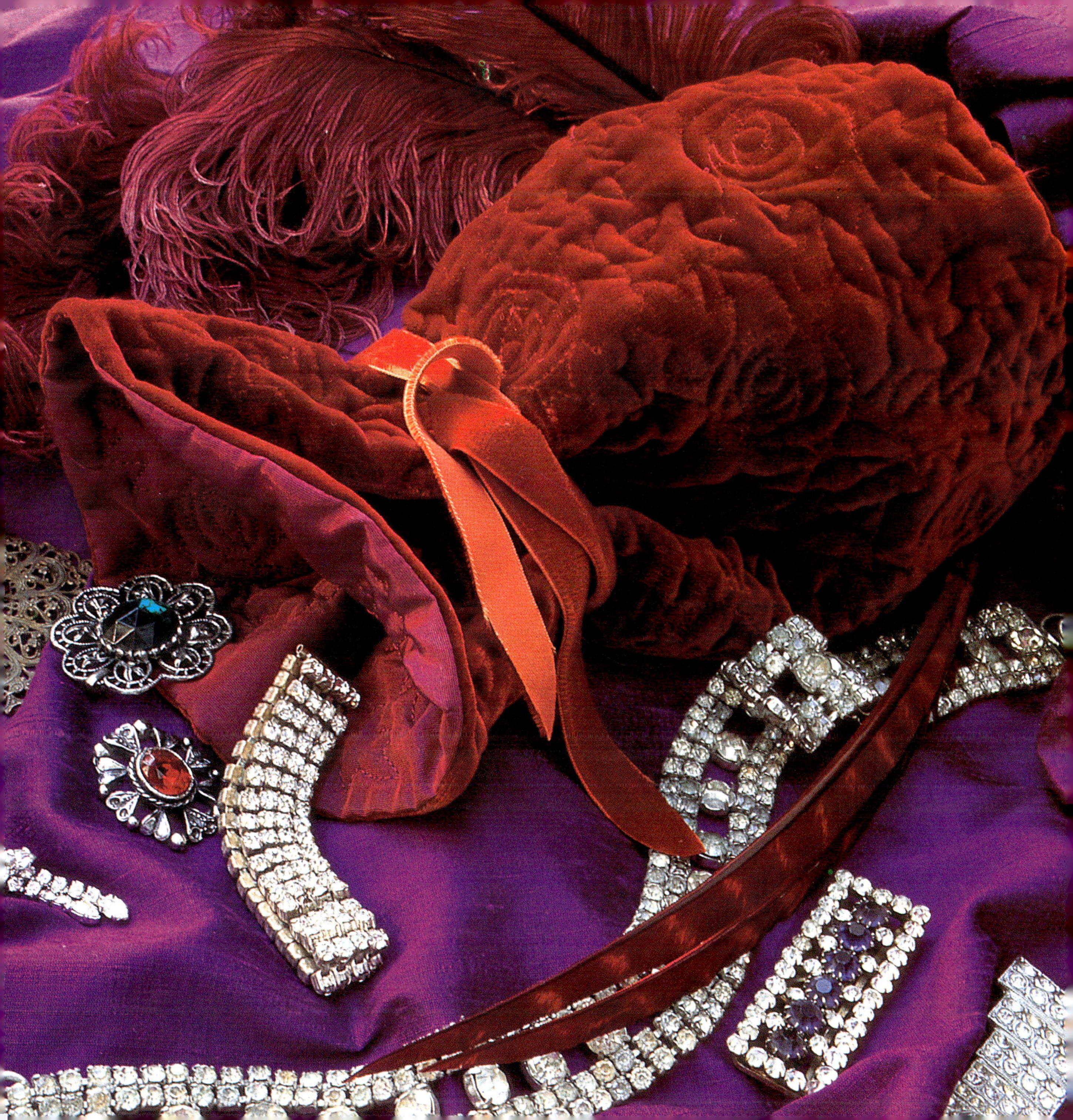

TEMPLATES

To enlarge the templates to the correct size, use either a grid system or a photocopier. For the grid system, trace the template and draw a grid of evenly spaced squares over your tracing. To scale up, draw a larger grid onto another piece of paper. Copy the outline onto the second grid by taking each square individually and drawing the relevant part of the outline in the larger square. Finally, draw over the lines to make sure they are continuous.

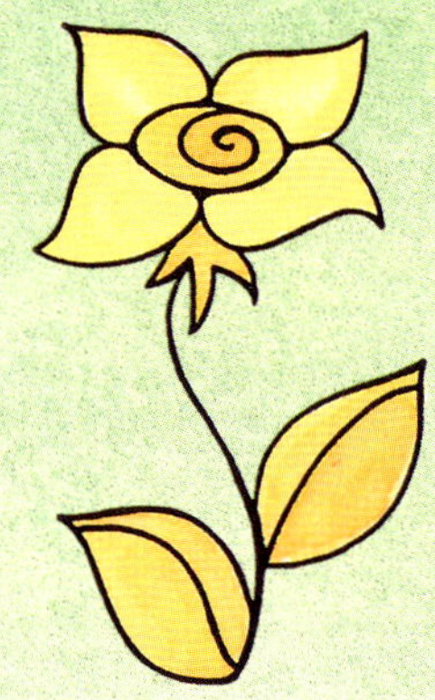

Rosebud-painted Pitcher, page 20

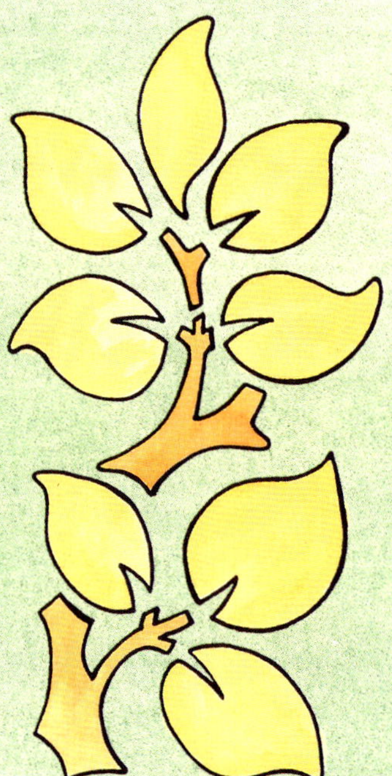

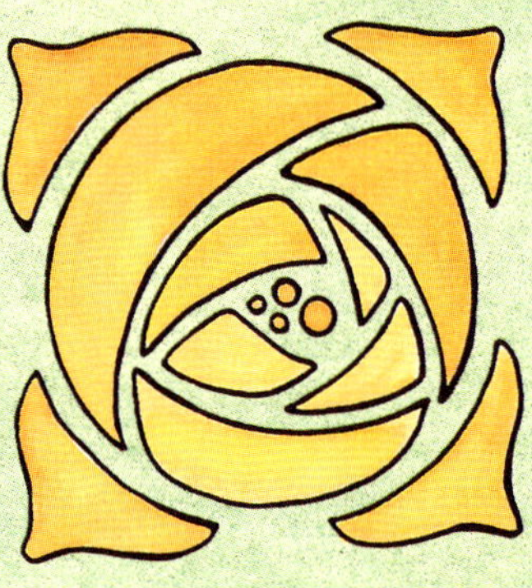

Rose-stenciled Tablecloth, page 50

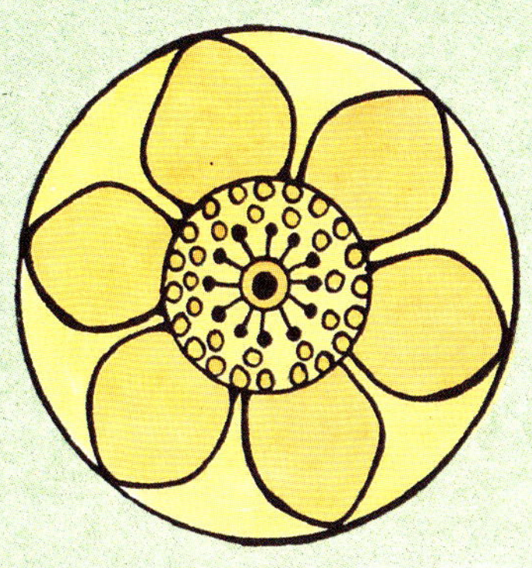

Wild Rose Chiffon Scarf, page 28

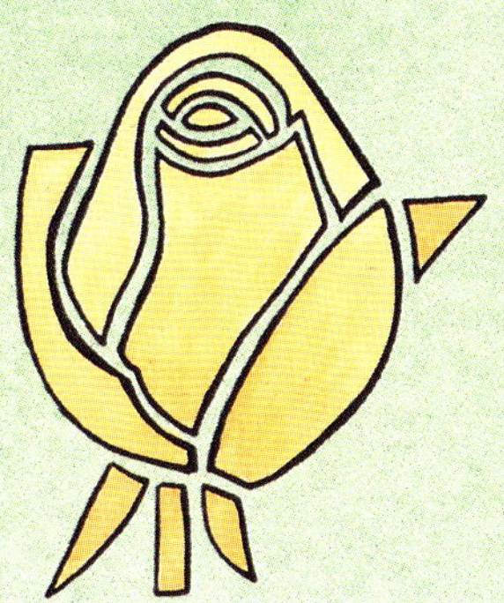

Yellow Roses Lampshade, page 18

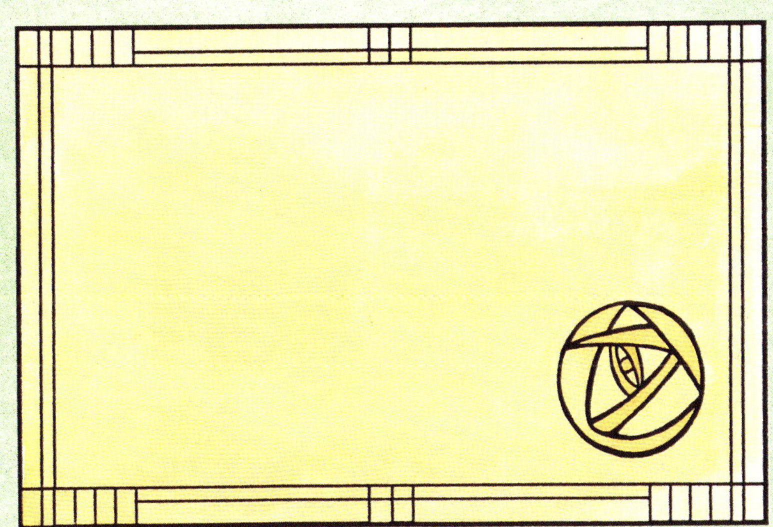

Water-resistant Rose Tablemat page 54

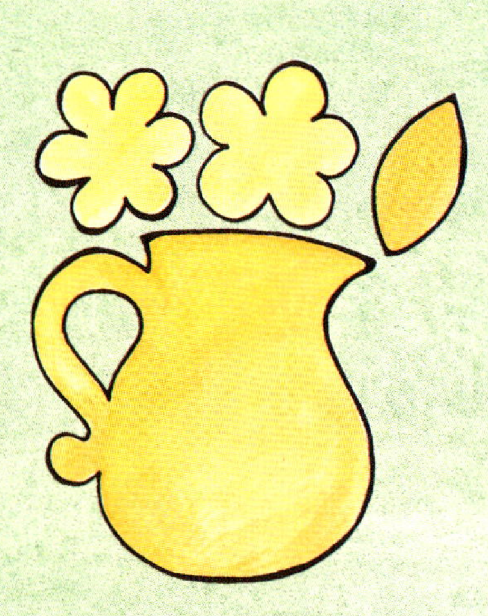

Rose Appliqué Bag, page 14

Rose-stamped Stationery, page 48

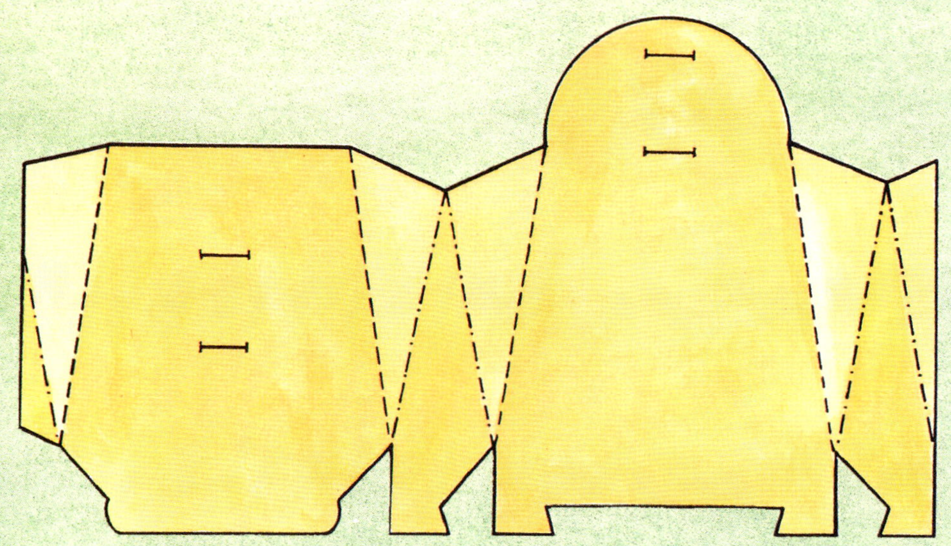

Rose-petal Confetti Box, page 38

Rose Jewelry Pouch, page 58

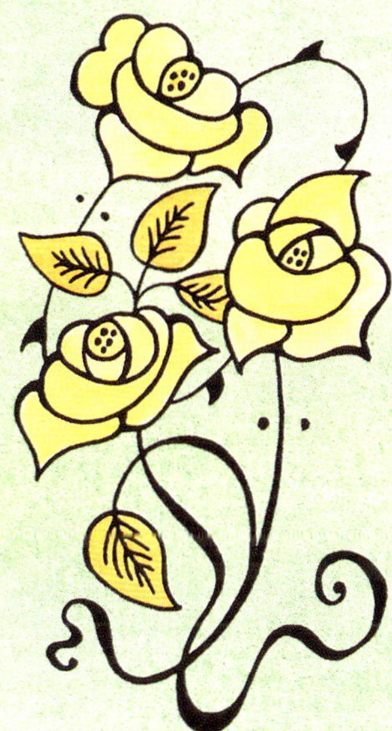

Art Nouveau Rose Box, page 36

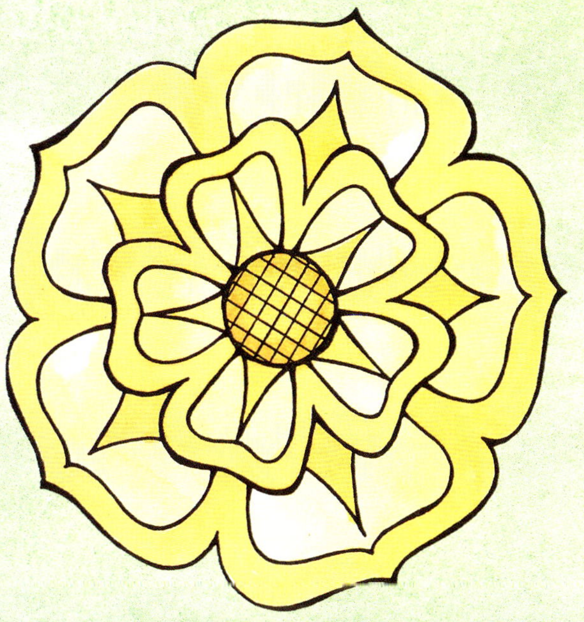

Tudor Rose Cushion page 40

ACKNOWLEDGMENTS

The author and publishers would like to thank the following people for designing the projects in this book:

Penny Boylan

Paper Roses Gift Box, p12
Satin Rose Hat Decoration, p24
Rose-stamped Stationery, p48

Lucinda Ganderton

Rose Appliqué Bag, p14
Decoupage Rose Eggs, p22
Rose Patchwork Throw, p30
Art Nouveau Rose Box, p36
Rose-stenciled Tablecloth, p50
Ribbon Rose Hairband, p56

Emma Petitt

Rosebud-painted Pitcher, p20

Isabel Stanley

Velvet Rose Coat Hanger, p26
Wild Rose Chiffon Scarf, p28
Rose-petal Confetti Box, p38
Sequinned Rose Bottle, p42
Rose Jewelry Pouch, p58

Dorothy Wood

Yellow Roses Lampshade, p18
Rose Brooch, p34
Tudor Rose Cushion, p40
Spray of Icing Rose, p44
Water-Resistant Rose Tablemat, p54

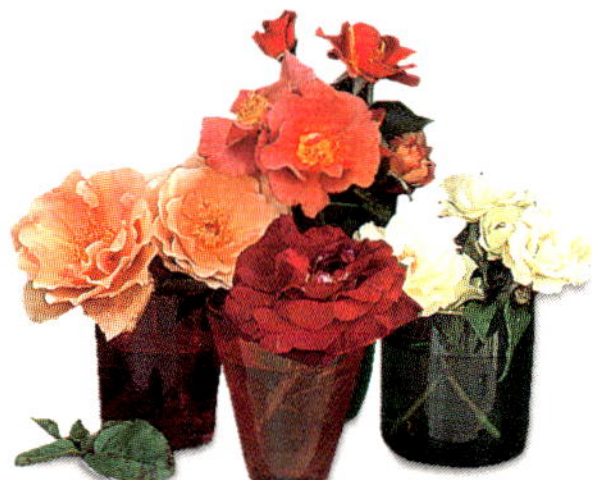

Picture Credits
The publishers would like to thank AKG Photo, London, for the use of the following photographs: p8 (top) *The Virgin in the Rose Bower* by Stephan Lochner, Wallraff-Richartz-Museum, Cologne, (bottom) *Mary in the Rose Arbour* by Martin Schongauer, St Martin's Minster, Colmar, p10 (top) *Rosebush*, a decorative panel by Ernest Quost, Musée d'Orsay, Paris, (bottom) *Venus Verticordia* by Dante Gabriel Rossetti, Russell Cotes Art Gallery, Bournemouth, p11 (top) *Bacchus with two Nymphs and Amor* by Caesar Beotius van Everdingen, Gemaeldegalerie, Alte Meister, Dresden.
Thanks also to The Bridgeman Art Library, London for the pictures on p9: *The Roses of Heliogabalus* by Sir Lawrence Alma Tadema, p11 (bottom) *Rose Design*, 1883, by William Morris, Victoria & Albert Museum, London.

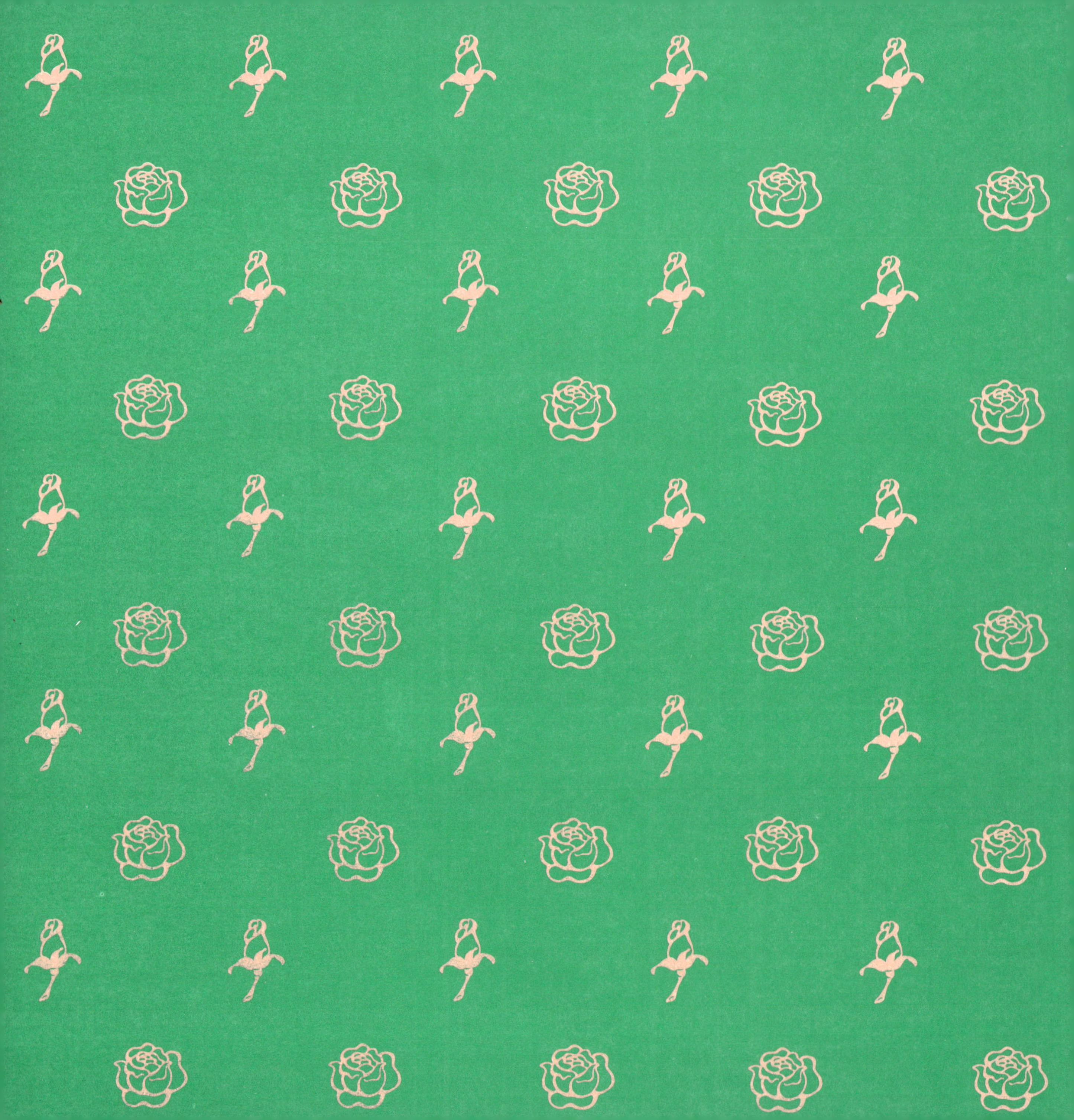